CRAZY
FAITH
Extravagant Love

CRAZY FAITH
Extravagant Love

RON AND CAROL
CANTRELL

PUBLISHED BY:
Inspired Creative Expressions, 370 Fenwick Dr., San Antonio, Texas 78239-2419

Printed in the United States of America
First Edition: July 2013

COVER DESIGN & LAYOUT: Ron Cantrell

Dedication

We dedicate this book to:

JESUS, Lover of our souls: Thank You for the great privilege to love You and Your people. Our lives are an offering to You.

HOLY SPIRIT: Thank you for nurturing and leading us to face-to-face encounters with Father's love and compassion.

OUR CHILDREN: Heather, Michael, and Raquel ("Shelly"), who were always up for the next crazy adventure with Dad and Mom somewhere in the world. We love you so much.

OUR SIX GRANDCHILDREN: This next crazy-faith mission adventure is for you! May you receive the full spiritual inheritance of your grandparents and go on to do greater exploits in the nations of the world. Your Geempa and Nama will be cheering you on to the finish line.

THE SENIOR LEADERS of THE MISSION CHURCH, Dave and Deb Crone, Dano and Regina McCollam, Gary and Karissa Hopkins: Thank you for patterning the presence-driven, joy-filled life, and providing an environment in which we could thrive, be refreshed, re-visioned, and re-launched. It is our great delight to run alongside you on this crazy faith journey.

Table of Contents

FOREWORD

Extravagant love does crazy things. It is the stuff great movies and epic novels are made of. The Bible is such a story: a Father bereaved of His children who will go to any length to get them back; a Son who suffers a tragic death to guarantee the life of His beloved bride; the Holy Spirit who transforms people by empowering them to taste of this unquenchable, eternal passion.

In this ancient love story, we find men and women who drink the intoxicating love of Heaven, and then begin to exhibit a nearly superhuman quality of life, with no regard for self-preservation, self-promotion, or selfish ambition. We find men and women, who, like Abraham, left the comfort zone of all that was familiar to follow an inward compass into the great unknown, because of crazy love. We find men like Moses who was compelled by the fires of burning love with a stick and a promise to deliver the oppressed from the mightiest nation of his day. Down through the ages crazy lovers face off with angry giants, ravenous lions, and battles of impossible odds. They suffered atrocities and serenely surrendered their bodies to the flames in the power and promise of crazy love. But crazy lovers are not limited to the time capsule of a finished biblical canon; they walk among us today.

I have had the honor of walking with some crazy lovers in the past thirty-five years of my spiritual journey, but rarely do we get to witness the encounters that mark their transformation. In this book, *Crazy Faith, Extravagant Love,* my dear friends, Ron and Carol Cantrell, let us glimpse into the courting parlor of their own heavenly romance. Through their stories and insights, we become witnesses to their personal transformation by the power of crazy love. I can also personally attest to the reality and depth of their continuing crazy love encounter. Ron beams with a contagious childlike wonder and faith that launches him into persecuted nations with the boldness from another world. Carol radiates the heavenly aroma of one who has poured out her costly ointment at the feet of Jesus in extravagant worship.

In this book you will find the voice of their story switching back and forth between Ron and Carol. This free-flow technique makes you feel like you are in a personal conversation with them. Their story is also powerfully practical by giving us glimpses of crazy faith and extravagant love in every aspect of life, from the prayer closet, to the work place; from touching individuals to impacting nations. My life has personally been enriched by my friendship with these two crazy lovers, and I believe yours will be as well. I pray that your love would abound more and more in depth and insight, and that you would know the love that surpasses knowledge. May you experience its heights, depths, width, and breadth and be forever changed by crazy faith through His extravagant love.

—Dan McCollam
Leader, The Mission Church, Vacaville, California
Author of *God Vibrations*

Listen!
You can be sure God is
speaking loud and clear
to you today.
So, be expectant,
lean in to hear Him, and
explore
the many ways He speaks.

INTRODUCTION

If we are out of our mind, it is for the sake of God; if we are in our right mind, it is for you. (2 Corinthians 5:13)

I was privileged to teach in Wales at a Bible School named after a martyred Welsh missionary to Korea, Robert Jermaine Thomas. They host "Celebration for the Nations" annually, a week of solid worship and prayer in their desire to re-dig the wells of revival that came from that small corner of the world a century ago. Teme, one of my students from Eritrea, gave me a journal as a parting gift. When I read the dedication he wrote inside, I just knew it had to be the title of this book.

> *Ron, I just want to say I love you. You are an amazing person. I love your simplicity and **crazy faith** you have in the Lord. It is a pleasure to know you! See you soon in East Africa. Your Brother, Teme.*

I could not get the phrase "crazy faith" out of my mind. To me it described perfectly the way my wife Carol and I have lived our lives. We see ourselves seated with Christ in heavenly places, being extravagantly embraced as we have sought to bring the world before His glorious splendor. Our lives, and the fruit of our labors, is our offering to Him, the reward of His sufferings.

To onlookers, the things that we have done in our 40 years of married life may have seemed crazy indeed. *Crazy Faith, Extravagant Love* recounts memorable testimonies and lessons of our journey with God. Our determination to walk with Jesus in complete faith has not been easy, but it has always been overshadowed by the Almighty every step of the way. Our personal journey of crazy faith has taken many turns, with trials that perhaps could have been avoided had we known then what we know now. Time, with its life experiences, is the best exercise of faith. In His great patience, God longs to bring us into His fullness. Our will, which He never transgresses, is that mighty seed of Him in us to make us like Him. His passionate pursuit strengthens and nurtures what He formed in us. As we journey with the Holy Spirit, we are not disqualified by our mistakes, failures, and weaknesses; we do not fail this life test! Rather, the Holy Spirit burns in us a resolve to know Him more intimately to mature in relationship with Him. With each encounter, we are transformed and radiate Jesus, shining with His brilliance, so that His name is glorified in all the earth. This is the purpose of the Great Commission.

Our wholehearted response to God's passionate pursuit appears, at times, crazy. I have often thought that the Apostle Paul must have been acting in a manner that suggested he was unbalanced spiritually. In Scripture, it is termed, "being beside himself," which led to the activities that launched vigorous apostolic ventures. In reality, his life was not balanced on any level. He never considered his dignity or how he appeared to others and gave no thought to his personal comfort or living conditions. In fact, the conditions he endured during his exploits for the sake of the Gospel were extreme to be sure: hunger, beatings, shipwreck, left for dead, no place to sleep, weeks of bone-weary travel, to name a few. He was a man driven by passion—the passion of someone who had seen his Messiah face-to-face.

Jesus is manifesting Himself again in echoes of those first century emissaries. A fresh wind is blowing over the earth right now. The Holy Spirit has the locked-on-gaze of literally thousands upon thousands of young people who are not satisfied with the status quo. Many of the older generation are feeling the wind as well, raising up their sails, and letting the ship run full-speed ahead with the younger warriors, finding renewed vigor in their bones. They are not seeing the present crisis conditions as a devastating storm, but as a Spirit-move that is filled with the favor of God sweeping them into a new era. Revolutionary change is on the horizon, and it is coming like a tidal wave.

Many are already being overwhelmed by God's goodness— that quality that made Moses' face shine like the sun. When Moses asked to see His glory, God gave him something so much better. He showed him His goodness, the very core of the Father's heart. The goodness of God is so powerful, He had to shelter Moses lest he die. Senior leader and Author, Bill Johnson, of Bethel Church in Redding, California, said: "You don't need strength to battle the devil; you need strength to contain the fire hurricane of the presence of God's love."[1] The strength that equips you to host His manifest presence causes the enemy camp intense pain and terrifying fear. They suffer great loss when God's goodness is poured out upon us and through us.

The Messiah, heretofore, left lonely by a tolerated level of unbelief in the Church, has responded to this awakening that is growing each day in intensity. Guilt-driven devotions are over; to-do lists of petitions for our Beloved to accomplish for us are passé. The mental picture of Jesus politely knocking on the door

---

[1]   Johnson, Bill. *Hosting the Presence of God*, Destiny Image, 2012.

of our hearts is being replaced by an ear-to-ear radiant grin as His Majesty runs headlong to claim His awakened Bride. Love is in the air, fueled by passion, and both Bridegroom and Bride have faces marked by deep satisfaction and intense joy.

Great joy! This word "joy," by the way, is mentioned in the Scriptures 165 times, whereas the word "sadness" only once. "Strength" appears 242 times, but, "weakness," just seven times. The word "sorrow" is only mentioned seven times in the New Testament. And yet, sadness, weakness, and sorrow have marked the Church for centuries as part of the normal Christian walk. It has become almost expected to live with weakness and suffering: "Well brother, it's just my weakness . . ." or, "This is my thorn in the flesh." Any "thorn in the flesh" or "weakness" has to be seen in a proper biblical view. The expectation of living as a suffering victim is indefensible from Heaven's perspective. The fact is, Jesus carried the weight of all our sin and suffering so that we might live in fullness of life through the resources afforded through His death and resurrection. God expects that we will pull from Heaven all we need to be fully equipped here on earth to run into the fray and win every battle. This is our inheritance as the saints.

> *I pray also that the eyes of your heart may be enlightened in order that you may know the hope to which he has called you, the riches of his glorious inheritance in the saints, and his incomparably great power for us who believe. That power is like the working of his mighty strength, which he exerted in Christ when he raised him from the dead...* (Ephesians 1:18-20)

Our inheritance is the same power God the Father used to raise Jesus from the dead! We are more than able to accomplish what God has given us to do.

Nothing held Paul back—not even his "thorn in the flesh."

And lest I should be exalted above measure by the abundance of the revelations, a thorn in the flesh was given to me, a messenger of satan to buffet me, lest I be exalted above measure. Concerning this thing I pleaded with the Lord three times that it might depart from me.

And He said to me, "My grace is sufficient for you, for My strength is made perfect in weakness." Therefore most gladly I will rather boast in my infirmities that the power of Christ may rest upon me. Therefore I take pleasure in infirmities, in reproaches, in needs, in persecutions, in distresses, for Christ's sake. For when I am weak, then I am strong. (2 Corinthians 12:7-10, NKJV)

Some have suggested that because Paul referred to his physical weakness, it is somehow meant for us to live by lower standards than Heaven actually intends, that we too should expect to succumb to limitations and tolerate weaknesses. Sadly, this has become the norm in Christian circles. Even Wikipedia,[2] the online encyclopedia, credits this phrase "thorn in the flesh" as a normal Christian colloquialism. The fact is, most people who use the "thorn in their flesh" as an excuse of weakness, or in mock humility, have not experienced such heavenly encounters to qualify their position. That is not the characteristic we want to be known by, in Heaven or on earth.

No other apostle mentioned a "thorn in the flesh," and for good reason. In the above section of Scripture, Paul explains why he was utterly dependent upon God's appropriated grace. Too often, the "suffering" of the body has been the focus, and yet Paul's emphasis was the lavish grace God provided in the

---

[2] Wikipedia, The Free Online Encyclopedia, www.wikipedia.org.

most extreme conditions. "Ecstasy beyond human ability" is the Greek word Paul used to describe Heaven's radiance upon him. He emphasized Christ's power manifested through his weakness. The suffering received by any thorns in our body is overwhelmingly eclipsed through the rich grace God gives to us. We only have to look at the fruit of Paul's life to affirm this.

The new blood-warriors being raised up in this hour are not satisfied to maintain the status quo—those things as they have been in our church history thus far. The fire hurricane of God's love, ramped up in intensity by His Holy Spirit, is arresting them. They are looking at our world with new eyes—eyes of crazy faith! They are leaping over the centuries, treating dogma like Olympic hurdles to get to the authentic Gospel of the apostles. Nothing is impossible for them, and that's not just a song they sing; it is their lifestyle. The litmus test of this new breed is, "When do we get to do greater things than Jesus did?" And they are doing them now, just as Jesus said they would.

Crazy faith celebrates before the answer comes.

> *Sing, O barren woman, you who never bore a child; burst into song, shout for joy, you who were never in labor; because more are the children of the desolate woman than of her who has a husband . . . Do not be afraid, you will not suffer shame . . . (Isaiah 54:1, 4)*

A barren woman sings and shouts her way to motherhood.

Crazy faith gives believers permission to explore all they are allowed to do and press through the limits to see just how far they are allowed to go while digging into the Father's tool box. The results are surprising as it seems there simply are no limits for those who trust Him fully. The fact is, the Holy Spirit has been waiting for such a generation. Some call them the "Joel 2 Army." I say it's much greater than that.

After 36 years in the ministry, Jesus revolutionized my

life by visiting me in a vision on Pentecost Sunday. Since that time, I mark my life as "before the awakening" and "since the awakening" because everything changed that dramatically.

The promise of Joel 2 is good, but it is by no means inclusive of all God is doing in this generation and the one coming. Crazy faith is shocking, core-shaking, earth-shattering, revolutionary, and at every turn, removing the spiritual cataracts from every eye to see the Kingdom with sharpened clarity like never before. It does not resemble what is considered the normal, "balanced" Christian life. Rather, it pushes the limits and taps into God's storehouse where the impossible becomes possible.

Full of Joy

In order to pursue the impossible, however, we need to live with the joy that Jesus promised His followers, "My joy I give you . . ." Why does He want us to live in joy? Because Heaven's primary atmosphere is celebrative joy. Have you considered that? Celebration is the full occupation of the angels and citizens of Heaven. C. S. Lewis wrote, "Joy is the very serious business of heaven."[3] What we have often done, unfortunately, is trade Heaven's joy, that relies solely and completely upon God and His resources, for the "seriousness" that is life on planet Earth. I'm determined to live in the reverse now. I told a team of Egyptian outreach warriors I had the pleasure of working with in Europe, "There is not one single thing on this earth to be serious about!" Then we exploded with joy. To live in such a way of surrendered joy means we have determined our lives will function only in Heaven's atmosphere, no matter what we face. This is, honestly, the only way to live.

Carol and I have a motto: "If it can't be done in joy, we're not doing it!" In other words, there is no other option for us! It becomes

---

[3] Lewis, C.S. *The Problem of Pain,* HarperCollins Publishers, 1940.

our attitude adjustment in any situation and our SOP[4] for any task or Kingdom mission at hand. Joy is the primary tool that transforms a gloomy, contentious, and miserable environment. We release joy when the tensions reach fever pitch—as demonic oppression threatens to silence, strangle, and disable us. Joy becomes our greatest weapon to break down the barriers and release captives. Joy sets people free. When joy is activated, everything of the opposite spirit dissipates and Heaven prevails.

Joy brings a celebration of life, and Jesus set the example for us.

> *Therefore, since we are surrounded by such a great cloud of witnesses, let us throw off everything that hinders and the sin that so easily entangles, and let us run with perseverance the race marked out for us. Let us fix our eyes on Jesus, the author and perfecter of our faith, who for the joy set before him endured the cross, scorning its shame, and sat down at the right hand of the throne of God.* (Hebrews 12:1, 2)

Jesus' last hours were marked by joy, not doom and gloom as is most often portrayed. We are His prize, after all, and that fills Him with great joy. Therefore, to live life celebratively is our mandate. You and I are the focus in this celebration, and the hosts of Heaven, with its grandstands filled with those who have gone before, are cheering us on toward our goal, Jesus.

> *Not that I have already attained, or am already perfected; but I press on, that I may lay hold of that for which Christ Jesus has also laid hold of me.*

---

[4]   SOP, standard operating procedure.

Brethren, I do not count myself to have apprehended; but one thing I do, forgetting those things which are behind and reaching forward to those things which are ahead, I press toward the goal for the prize of the upward call of God in Christ Jesus. (Philippians 3:12-14, NKJV)

This is not the "last word" on crazy faith, nor is it conclusive. It has really only just begun. Our testimony written here is to encourage many to run further and faster, to get caught up in this adventurous jet stream.

Then the LORD answered me and said, "Write the vision . . . that he may run who reads it." (Habakkuk 2:2, NKJV)

If you listen closely, you can hear the scrambling of the communication systems within the enemy camp out of sheer terror because of what they know is about to descend upon their centuries-held strongholds. But don't focus long on the enemy's camp—God's song of "you" is being played. The angels are in a choreographed celebration dance over your role in this time in history. You won't want to miss one single beat!

I'm going through
this door—
the passage into a
secret garden of
delights and surprises—
my hiding place
away from it all . . .

ONE

HEAVEN ON EARTH

Immediately I was in the Spirit, and a throne was set there in heaven. One was seated on the throne, and the One seated looked like jasper and carnelian stone. A rainbow that looked like an emerald surrounded the throne . . . Flashes of lightning and rumblings of thunder came from the throne . . . (Revelation 4:2-3, 5a)

I lost count of how many times I listened to the "Revelation Song." It was impacting me in a way that went deep into my spirit. As I played the song in a loop again and again, the power of its words seemed to just take me away as I basked in God's presence now permeating the atmosphere of my home office. Each word of the "Revelation Song" seemed Holy Spirit-chosen and anointed, with no wasted thoughts, just a masterpiece of song writing.

Revelation Song[5]

Worthy is the Lamb who was slain
Holy, holy is He
Sing a new song to Him who sits on
Heaven's mercy seat

Holy, holy, holy is the Lord God Almighty
Who was and is and is to come
With all creation I sing praise to the King of kings
You are my everything and I will adore You

Clothed in rainbows of living color
Flashes of lighting, rolls of thunder
Blessing and honor, strength and glory and power be
To You the only wise King

Filled with wonder, awestruck wonder
At the mention of Your name
Jesus Your name is power, breath and living water
Such a marvelous mystery

After a time, I felt that sitting in my chair just seemed disrespectful to the strong presence I was feeling. I rose to my feet, hands in the air, and continued to be lost in worship. God's presence became thicker, unsettling my equilibrium, when uncontrollably, I sank down onto my knees. Eyes closed, hands raised to Heaven as worship leader Kari Jobe sang out, "Filled with wonder, awestruck wonder, at the mention of Your Name…"

The truth of those words suddenly transported me somewhere

---

[5] "Revelation Song" by Jennie Lee Riddle, ©2004 Gateway Create Publishing (Admin. By Integrity's Praise! Music). All Rights reserved. International copyright secured. CCLI song #4447960.

else. A scene began to unfold before my eyes as half of my office disappeared.

Heavenly Vision

To the horizon, I could see an unfathomable myriad of people standing in a semicircle before the mountain of the Lord. "Heaven!" I thought to myself as I viewed this breathtaking scene. There was a soft, amber glow as if the lights had been turned down. No one was praising; rather, they were standing with awe and expectation. I did not see the "bright light" that so many speak of, nor did I hear the thunderous sounds of Heaven's ongoing worship and singing. Momentarily, I was aware of the presence of Jesus on the outcropping of stone. The amber haze obscured Him, but He was there along with an inexplicable knowledge of His beauty and supreme perfection that flooded my being with the force of a tsunami wave.

The power of this vision of the Throne room sat me flat down on my office floor as wave after wave hit me. God's Being was so overwhelming that my body began shaking uncontrollably as I felt myself being pressed down until I was facedown on the floor.

"My God . . . I am undone!" was all I could whisper as I lay prostrate before the revelation of His Majesty, violently trembling with the currents that surged through my body. Kari Jobe continued to sing out her worship on my laptop somewhere in the distance.

Time passed with me there on the floor, I don't know how long. Copious tears were now gushing from my eyes as was the question from my heart: *How can One like You be concerned with me? I am nothing!*

My mind struggled with this reality. In the nearness of His presence, everything I had ever done suddenly looked like a pile of ashes. A Scripture flashed through my mind from the book of Revelation that I knew described the Church at Laodicea,

27

"wretched, miserable, poor, blind, and naked." Partial phrases came from my lips in strained whispers as I attempted to rise, "Why me. . .? How could You care . . .? Who am I . . .?"

I struggled back to my knees and attempted to lift my hands to a posture of praise, but they would only rise up halfway. Then another wave from the mountain washed over me and pinned me unmovable, frozen, mouth gaping open, arms at half-mast, and shaking all over. Struggling just to breathe, I could only catch short gulps mixed with cries, "God help me!" I would catch my breath just in time for another wave to overtake me again, attempt to recover, struggle to breathe, weep, gasp, and question God again. This was repeated over and over.

Jesus Speaks

I finally cried out in desperation between the shock waves, "What is this?"

There was a long, silent pause, and then the simple answer came softly, serenely, almost in a whisper from the Rock, "This is eye salve so you can see Me as I really am."

How can you not see, and yet see? I thought to myself. The amber haze was still there obscuring Him, and yet I saw Him as He really is in eternity. The vision of perfection manifested before me caused everything else to be as rubbish in comparison. Other biblical characters that saw God in similar revelations flashed through my mind and I recalled that they made a confession of being "undone," and in this moment before His glory, I understood why.

I am undone, was all my heart could say at the revelation before me. *I am completely undone . . .*

My weeping was not quiet; it was wracking sobs so loud that I thought I would awaken my wife who was fast asleep across the hall. By now it was well past midnight. Struggling to rise up,

I went to see if Carol was still asleep and was relieved that my loud weeping had not awakened her.

In a drunken stupor, I stumbled downstairs as I considered what I had just seen, as waves of God's presence continued to crash over my body and soul. With each wave, I struggled to breathe, crumpled to the floor violently shaking, and all I could do was respond in worship to His glorious majesty. The scene of the Throne room remained permanently vivid, burned into my soul. Whenever I closed my eyes, there was Jesus before me and the words He spoke so gently to my heart.

Time stood still. My legs and arms felt like someone had poured in lead. Laying on my back on the living room floor, tears threatened to fill up my ears. Four hours had passed so quickly in the presence of the Lord. Somewhere after 2:00 AM, I finally stumbled to bed.

Awakened

The next morning I arose unusually early even though I had gone to bed so late. My wife found me outside sitting on our patio reading the Bible. I continued to reel from the waves of His glory which had resumed once I awoke. Through sobbing cries and copious tears, I attempted to explain to her what had happened during the night.

"I sensed a change when you came to bed," she told me. "I felt the weighty presence of God and all I could do was respond in deep adoration for two hours. I also felt a powerful, new authority of God upon you," she told me.

Undone

We sat on the porch for hours as I recounted the events of the night. For the past year and a half, Carol had been experiencing a personal revival, so she understood the intensity of fresh desire this awakening created in me. From time to time, I would have to abandon our conversation and rush to my office upstairs, swept away again by tidal waves of powerful manifestations of God's presence. I was concerned that the intensity of His presence would cease—that this might be just a one-off experience without a lasting effect. I did not want the weightiness of His presence to ever leave me, for never had I tasted such sweetness. I felt like I was reborn all over again.

"The most important thing you can do right now," Carol urged, "is to be very, very responsive to the gentle wooing of the Holy Spirit as you feel Him call you away for communion." As I did, I found I was able to soak in the ocean of His healing presence, creating an environment of habitation for the Lover of my soul.

Over the following days I would join Carol for short discussions, but only in between debilitating surges of God's glorious presence on me. I was living in an "undone" state. At times I felt like I could not breathe correctly, and most of the time, I could barely stand up on my feet. To do so, I had to brace myself to keep from falling to the floor. My trembling, weak legs just would not hold me up. It was easier, actually, to fall before His presence and lay in adoration as waves of His love were transforming and healing me. Whenever I closed my eyes, I saw the Throne of God and heard Jesus' voice, and once again, I would be swept away to that place of worship before Him. Indeed, I was learning to respond to His presence in humility and worship, much like the citizens of Heaven do continually.

The Presence of Angels

Ron and I felt the presence of angels in our house during those weeks—not only in the house, and in our car, but everywhere we went. One day as I was praying, God showed me two massive warrior angels, each with a blinding brilliance, who had been assigned to us. We felt them guarding what God had initiated. The power and presence of Heaven's atmosphere was particularly tangible in our home. Friends and family who visited us following the vision said they sensed such peace—the shalom of God. Heaven's atmosphere was permeating our lives with powerful manifestation of His presence.

Heaven's Eternal Song

The intensity of the heavenly vision with its shock waves drove me (Ron) to the book of Revelation from which the song that had caused my facedown response had been inspired. Turning to the words of Jesus' beloved disciple John, the proclamations of adoration almost leapt off the pages. In John's summons to Heaven as recorded in chapter four, he saw the four living creatures crying, "Holy, holy, holy, is the Lord God Almighty." I now understood why the elders were compelled to fall prostrate before the presence of God's revealed glory.

It seems that heavenly visions create hunger for more God-encounters and more revelation from His Word. I was enjoying a new level of intimate communion and friendship with God as I worshiped Him day and night. In light of God's glorious presence on me, I vowed to never bring His Majesty a list of items I expected Him to do. Instead, the rest of my life will be devoted to adoring Him.

Eyesight Prescription

During the throes of the tsunami waves of His glory that washed over me, I asked the Lord, *What is this?* Jesus answered, "Eye salve."

> *I advise you to buy from Me gold refined in the fire so that you may be rich, white clothes so that you may be dressed and your shameful nakedness not exposed, and ointment to spread on your eyes so that you may see.* (Revelation 3:18, NKJV)

Realizing the state of my blindness, the most important follow up question was, *How do I buy eye salve to cure my condition?* That became one of my pleadings to the Lord as the waves continued . . . *With what currency could I possibly purchase the heavenly items listed here to the Laodicean church?*

Pentecost Sunday

My vision took place late Sunday night, June 1, 2009, and into the early hours of Monday. Carol pointed out that God chose to reveal Himself on Pentecost Sunday, or *Shavuot*, as it is known in Hebrew. The biblical Feast of Shavuot commemorates God demonstrating His terrifying power and majesty to the Israelites in the wilderness at Sinai with dark clouds, fire, and thunderings. This was also the feast when the Holy Spirit fell upon those gathered in the Upper Room.

> *When the day of Pentecost had arrived, they were all together in one place. Suddenly a sound like that of a violent rushing wind came from heaven, and it filled the whole house where they were staying. And tongues, like flames of fire that were divided, appeared to them and rested on each one of them. Then they were all filled with the Holy Spirit and began to speak in different languages, as the Spirit gave them ability for speech.* (Acts 2:1-4, HCSB)

I felt it so appropriate that the Lord chose this day to reignite His fire deep in my heart.

Never Again Normal

By Friday, June 5, I had not recovered to a "normal" state by any means. I was still trembling, very weepy, and weakened as I meditated in His presence. I now understood the prophets' words of feeling completely "undone" when they described their encounters with the Living God. For several days, I was unable to drive the car any significant distance without breaking down and weeping uncontrollably. When the waves came, I would involuntarily close my eyes so I could see Heaven again, and that can hinder driving—or walking, for that matter.

I determined in those days that I never wanted to be "normal" again. For me, the "normal" state had become a miserable, and unsatisfying place to live. Living before the presence of the Lord in all I do for Him would become the highest priority of my life. To this day, all other activities pale in comparison. I have no desire to return to the place where duty and service takes precedence over living in an intimate relationship with Him. Carol and I have both resolved to live this way: surrendered completely to the Spirit of God with clarity of vision and attuned hearing. Over 40 years ago, we volunteered to be employed full time by the Lord of the harvest for His purposes in the nations. Following the vision, we re-surrendered our lives afresh.

Revived

In light of the visitation from the Lord, I sought to read all the scriptural accounts and books about personal God-encounters and past revivals. I came across Joy Dawson's book, *The Fire of God*.[6] In the chapter called "Preparation for Revival Fire," she clarifies some of the dynamics of what I had experienced.

---

[6] Dawson, Joy. *The Fire of God*, Destiny Image, 2005.

When we experience the fire of God's power on our bodies, we may lie down on the floor on our backs, face up. Sometimes there is great change in one or more areas of our lives. But, sometimes there is relatively little change to our spiritual lives. The children of Israel saw God's breathtaking power in epic proportions, but it never changed their lives. Whereas, when we are exposed to more than an average degree of God's holiness [as in my vision], *we usually lie prostrate on the floor, face down. It was so with Daniel the prophet and the apostle John and the prophet Ezekiel who had those sort of encounters with Almighty-ness.*[7] *And those encounters had by far the most life changing results.*

The difference, Dawson points out, is seeing God's power (face up) and seeing God's holiness (face down). She continues:

In genuine revival, God does more to extend His Kingdom in seconds or minutes than in days, weeks, months, or years of God-inspired and energized Christian activity and teaching. The course of history toward righteousness can be changed in a nation quicker than any other way through genuine revival.

I must comment on Dawson's observation. Revival launched by a vision of God's holiness will always involve repentance and restitution. Those two God-blessed sisters of holiness will solidify the life and heart transformation that we long for. I did not want the powerful effect of my vision to fade. I determined to press in and, with an ever-burning desire, go as far as God would allow me to go and never return to that old state.

---

[7] See Dan. 10, Ezek. 2:22, Rev. 1:9-16.

Fear and Awe of God

If I were to characterize this encounter with God it would be "fear" and "awe." Any biblical account of a face-to-face encounter with God always brought a fresh revelation of Who He is, and fear and awe is always the response. Without the fear of God activated in our lives, we substitute religious practices and culture for His living presence.

The prophet Jeremiah uses a unique word when describing the condition of his backslidden nation:

> *Consider then and realize how evil and bitter it is for you when you forsake the LORD your God and have no **awe** of me," declares the Lord, the LORD Almighty.* (Jeremiah 2:19, emphasis mine)

The word "awe" that is used is the form of a Hebrew word *pachad* and is used only this one time in Scripture. It is stronger than the word normally used for "fear" and is more like "dread" inferring much more than a reverential fear of God. Most of the epiphanic scriptural visitations of the Lord that I could recall had visible manifestations that could be diagnosed as symptoms of this kind of dread (*pachad*): Daniel,[8] the prophet Ezekiel,[9] Isaiah,[10] Saul[11] of Tarsus, John seeing the ascended Messiah in His glory,[12] the priests who experienced God's glory filling the temple are just a few.

The worship song, "Beautiful,"[13] bears a line that arrests my heart: "Here, in Your presence, I am not afraid of brokenness..."

---

[8] Dan. 8:17, 18:27-10:7-19.

[9] Ezek. 1:1-27.

[10] Isa. 6:1-8.

[11] Acts 9:4.

[12] Rev. 1:17.

[13] "Beautiful," by Kari Jobe, copyright 2008, Gateway Worship.

"Brokenness" and "judgment" are something to be feared and are full of terrifying dread to those who have not experienced God's loving and mercifully forgiving presence. However, to those who have experienced His beautiful presence, they are much welcomed and desired. The fact is, there is no condemnation to a repentant and broken heart, but rather, only a burning love and the welcome, open arms of the Master of Heaven.

Life-Transforming God-Encounters

God-encounters of this magnitude become the pivotal points that change the course of our lives. We are transformed by God, and He then transforms others through our personal testimony of the encounter. Our life then becomes the catalyst to release breakthrough to others.

Scripture continually presses us to seek the Lord while He may be found.[14] God will always urge us to press in to Him, in times of peaceful conditions and during the most difficult moments of our life. If we have been exercised during peaceful times, it will be easier to find Him when everything seems to be going wrong and falling apart.

This injunction to seek God comes with an assurance that He has every intention to meet us and encounter us with a life-transforming engagement that will enlarge our heart to receive the revelation of His character for all we need. I (Carol) have found that at my most desperate times, as I have sought the Lord for answers, He is already waiting to impart revelation, healing, hope, inspiration, with an enlarged capacity to love Him. The nearness of His presence fills me with a profound gratitude for Who He is for me as I respond to His invitation into a deeper relationship. We come to appreciate that a distressing life issue, and our journey through it, often becomes encouragement

---

[14]   Isa. 55:6.

to scores of people in similar circumstances. These intimate God-moments, where we are the most vulnerable, are meant to strengthen us, and, in turn, release strength to others. The revelation of God's character in the intense circumstance will be the grace we live on in the next moments, and He is always more than enough.

Moses, too, depended upon God's character to sustain him. He had many life-transforming God-encounters that built his faith, encouraged his doubting heart, and strengthened and empowered him. He went, in the strength of those face-to-face encounters with God to engage head-on with some of the strongest demonic displays of witchcraft ever seen on the earth.

We are utterly dependent upon God's presence to empower us as we seek Him, find Him, and encounter Him. No matter the intensity of the challenges we face today, God will meet us with the strength of His character through an intimate exchange.

The Generals

I (Ron) continued to dig with my intense desire to understand "revival" in the lives of those who had experienced something similar to what had just happened to me. I came across a couple of books that brought greater understanding: *God's Generals*,[15] and *Deeper Experiences of Famous Christians*.[16] I was hungry to know more about what led them to a renewed abandonment in loving God and the outflow result of compassionate love in service to people.

I (Carol) had a similar God encounter to Ron's in 1988. God surprised me as I was leading worship and was lost in His presence

---

[15]   Liardon, Roberts. *God's Generals*, Whitaker House Publishers, 2003.

[16]   Gilchrist, Lawson J. *Deeper Experiences of Famous Christians*, Glad Tidings Publishing Company, 1911.

at a congregational retreat. It felt more like I was knocked off my feet as Heaven's joy exploded over me. One moment I was leading worship for a room full of people, and the next moment I was on the ground overwhelmed by Him. It seemed like every cell in my being was responding to God's powerful presence and the result was intense, overflowing joy. My only response was to laugh uncontrollably from a very deep place within me as waves of joy erupted, healing me from the inside out.

What happened over the coming minutes, hours, days and years was a complete transformation and personal breakthrough in every area of my life—health and healing of body, peace in soul and spirit, and a fresh calling and anointing to lead worship. Three years later, God launched Ron and I back to Israel to work for another 16 years.

The proof of any encounter with God is always the fruit. I was living Heaven's atmosphere and releasing it everywhere. What characterized my encounter with God at this time was intense joy—Heaven's joyous ecstasy—and it was being released with every action of my life.

Wholly Consecrated

While Carol was on one of her trips to Japan, she received a gift from a pastor expressing his gratitude for her ministry there. When she examined the little black book upon her return to Jerusalem, she discovered that it was over 100 years old and had originated in Springfield, Missouri. *Deeper Experiences of Famous Christians* became her treasure because of its content— those who had come to deeper experiences of the Holy Spirit— and it was a reminder of her own obedience to serve God in the nations, no matter the cost.

I was captivated by the testimonies recorded in the little black book as I compared my own experience on Pentecost Sunday. I was especially carried away and transfixed by John

Bunyon's experience with Jesus that caused him to write *Pilgrim's Progress*, which has been translated into every major language.

One morning, Carol and I considered the long journey of this little book. It made its way from the region of my parents and grandparents in the state of Missouri, across the ocean to Japan, all the way to Jerusalem with Carol, and returned back to America, carrying the testimonies of God's glory in the lives of men. Now here we were being inspired by those who had encountered the presence of God in such powerful, life-transforming ways.

The real weight of this comes from my grandparents whose lives were transformed from the "brush arbor" revival meetings in Missouri in the early 1900s. I have so many memories of my grandmother, Lucy, who would be so overcome by the presence of God through the Holy Spirit, she would worship Him unashamedly and demonstratively wherever she was. I would see her suddenly respond to the Holy Spirit as she stepped away from her cook stove, whirl around the kitchen in a glory dance, then resume her cooking. My father and mother were greatly impacted by this same revival and went on to serve as circuit-riding revivalists in Missouri many years prior to my birth. Later, they pastored an Assembly of God church in Missouri.

God had reserved this moment following my amazing encounter with Him to discover this book so that I could really value my own spiritual heritage. It caused me to appreciate all the years leading up to this moment as well as trusting what He has planned for my future.

There is a signature inside the cover from someone named George C. Batson. He penned something that I can only give God great thanks for and simply say, "Amen." Some words are missing, but you'll get the message:

. . . . the end of my earthly . . .

. . . . enter into the joy . . .

. . . . thus, with Thy great . . .

. . . . may I regain Thy favor . . .

. . . . blessing to the humility of . . .

The end of the inscription is clearer with fewer words missing:

Please, O Holy God, please, make me a man after Thine own heart and fulfill all Thy will as Thou has put Thy trust in me. Amen. George Charles Batson.

Batson's prayer truly describes what Carol and I have given ourselves to through the years: to love God with all of our hearts and to fulfill His heart's desires in the nations of the earth. We have determined to live in an intimacy of relationship with God where Heaven is touching Earth through us, staying loosely attached to anything that would hold us back from an immediate response to the Holy Spirit.

God would only allow me to grieve in repentance over my years of neglecting this relationship for a short time and then He told me clearly, "This is not the atmosphere of Heaven. There is only joy up here. Now I want you to enter deeply into My joy—the joy that I have especially prepared for you." Experiencing this kind of joy can only be through an intimate friendship with God. Being marked by Heaven's joy has propelled Carol and I into a place we never before imagined.

Since my vision, I have to say that the fire is stronger, the vision of Heaven sharper, and the purposes for that visitation of God are seen with much more clarity for the work to do in this hour. With everything in us, Carol and I have determined this season of our life will be more fruitful than all those previous.

Our mandate is to encourage the Bride to walk in her glorious and victorious identity, to draw closer in intimate relationship with her Bridegroom, destroy the works of the enemy, and take back captives from the grip of satan. These are our marching orders.

We determine to release Heaven's atmosphere of love's fire and passion here on Earth.

You pretend to sleep
beside me
that my shy eyes
may explore you.
I perceive that your heartbeat
is not that of
one who sleeps.

LOVE'S FIRE AND PASSION

Lord, take my heart and never give it back to me.
Why was I born if not to love you passionately?

> —*A prayer by Bishop Vladimir Ghica of Romania,*
> *persecuted in Russia.*

What moves Heaven? What is it that God cannot resist? Over what do angels gather in breathless wonder? The answer is so simple: extravagant love. It is the very essence of God's nature manifested to those He is so passionate about here on Earth, and then this love and passion is returned back to Him as a fervent worship response. God's love burns with Heaven's fire which then ignites our hearts to surrender completely to His overtures. It is His passion that causes us to zealously honor all people and find practical ways to release God's love through our lives laid down as we wash the feet of the very next person we encounter.

Love's fire and passion will always be the driving force and prime motivator to satisfy God's heart and seek to right the injustices perpetrated on earth.

An unusual outpouring of love evokes an extravagant response. In the early '70s, during the Jesus People Movement, I had a wild encounter with the Person of Jesus, which I never knew was possible. My erroneous mental image of Him was destroyed by the Truth. The hungry love pursuit during the '60s with the hippie movement triggered God's responsive heart with a revival wave of His pure love that circled the globe. Carol and I are both products of this wave. The amazing Father-heart of God was discovered by a generation suffering with serious father-issues. The hippies' intense desire for genuine love expressions caused God to come running, arms open, blowing the gates of Heaven right off their hinges.

Modern Love Surge

The present outpouring of love is stronger and, I believe, more daring. Today, tens of thousands gather together out their of passion for Jesus. Numerous cities in the USA have regular annual or biannual gatherings that draw upward of 25,000 youth set on fire for Jesus. This phenomena is not exclusive to America. The "Cave Church" in Egypt drew 70,000 on the Global Day of Prayer in Cairo on "11-11-11." That was a spiritual earthquake in this Islamic nation, the seed of the Kingdom in the belly of the dragon.

Prayer rooms that operate 24/7 now dot Europe through a movement started by the British Christian minister Pete Greig and author of *Red Moon Rising*. Worship and prayer has carried on unceasing for more than 13 years at the International House of Prayer in Kansas City, Kansas.[17] There, live worship bands take

---

[17] IHOP-KC, under the directorship of Mike Bickle.

two-hour sets, and at least one instrument is playing at all times so that the worship before God's presence never ceases. Tens of thousands of radical lovers gather in "extreme" worship for days on end to celebrate together at events such as "Jesus Culture." And, thousands are turned out annually into the marketplace and ministries from intensive training schools as patterned by Bethel Church in Redding, California, now replicated around the world.

There is a growing passion for Jesus that is causing our young people to radically invade every sphere of society with the Spirit's fire and love for the peoples of all nations with a burning desire to right the injustices of this world. They have been ignited and deployed by the Spirit of God with His compassionate and healing love. God cannot resist this outpouring, nor would He want to. You can feel the thrill in the heavens at responsive hunger. God's extravagant response is stronger and more dangerous because He is true to His faithful nature. We can expect, therefore, our nation will encounter God's transforming power as His lovers cry out before Him.

The Shadow Lands of Dullness

God's love has been characterized as a raging, fire hurricane. For our own protection, it seems, we are encased in a cocoon of dullness, a place that I call "the shadow lands," where the trials and troubles of earth, with its mundane tasks and boring, repetitive exercises of our material world leave us wondering, *What is this all really about? Is this all there is?* However, from time to time, the Holy Spirit will slice the cocoon open for a glimpse of the fire of God as He offers us a key with which we can open a door of access to that fire hurricane. Scales are falling off the eyes and cocoons are being abandoned for something sweeter than anything we have ever tasted. Like the Psalmist said, "Taste and see that the Lord is good."[18] He is indeed.

Meanwhile, Heaven seeks to break through with passion. Small glimpses happen periodically: stirred emotions during a particular worship song, a really good message at church that releases some degree of the genuine atmosphere of Heaven, an email with a powerful testimony, etc. Even so, we warn ourselves with statements like, "One can't be so heavenly minded that he is no earthly good," lest we get carried away. "Good Christians are balanced Christians," we try to convince ourselves.

Loving God . . . Wholly

Jesus' answer to the inquiry about the greatest commandment by the Pharisee, an expert in the Law, was shocking. He responded to this hungry one, "Love . . . with all your heart, and all your soul, and all your mind."[19] The Law says, "With all your heart, and all your soul, and all your strength...,"[20] but the word "mind" is not mentioned in the original Old Testament law. Jesus was saying, a heart completely given over to God is the greatest commandment. He was challenging the Pharisee to come up to a higher level of love rather than merely keeping a religious law. Why? Because the mind, the intellect, had become an idol to the Pharisees. They had taken the laws of God given through Moses and enlarged them by making lengthy commentary upon the simplicity of what God actually required, and in the process left no room for God's mercy. These intellectual renderings of God's merciful ways through the Law had become heavy, cruel burdens His people could no longer live by. In Jesus' time, they looked nothing like what God had originally intended. He exposed their motives and unmerciful ways again and again.

---

[18] Ps. 34:8.

[19] Matt. 22:37, NIV.

[20] Deut. 6:5.

In this particular interaction with the Pharisee, an expert in Judaic Law, Jesus urges him to love God wholeheartedly and gives no foothold to the intellect. He then poses a question on Messiahship so complex that it left the proud keepers of the Law speechless. "Whose Son is the Messiah?" Jesus inquired. Then he asked a follow-up question, "If he is the son of David, how is it that David calls Him Lord?"[21]

Never again did the elite Pharisaical leadership question Jesus on such subjects.

The Unbalanced Life of Jesus

I find little "balance" in the life of Jesus. On a regular basis, He confronted issues that had become a normal way of living the balanced Jewish life, and yet those keeping the Law were far from living in relationship with the Father as He intended. Jesus Himself lived what seemed to be contrary to the Law. For instance, He spoke to a Samaritan woman *alone* in a public place; He allowed a woman to anoint His feet with oil; He broke most of the Pharisaical laws; He did not insist that His disciples follow the rabbinic standards of what was considered "holy" living; He "worked" on the Sabbath and publicly announced that His Father worked on the Sabbath as well.

Jesus established the priority of a loving relationship with Father and patterned a life that pleased Him. He demonstrated Heaven's perspective on what "balance" really looks like.

Balance is overturning a city you are visiting.

These men who have turned the world upside down have come here too. (Acts 17:6, HCSB)

---

[21] Matt. 22:42-43.

Balance is being so marinated in Jesus that people actually accuse you of acting just like Him.

> *And they took note that these men had been with Jesus.* (Acts 4:13)

Jesus did not lead a balanced life, nor did He teach His disciples to be balanced, neither in His personal interaction with God or His treatment of the Law interpretations of His day. In fact, Jesus may have intentionally broke most of the rabbinic laws because they had become men's traditions. By this time, keeping the laws had little to do with the Law of Moses. Jesus refused to even identify with rabbinic laws. My good friend, Yossi Pollinger, an Israeli Jewish believer, said:

> *Jesus even called leaders of the law out into truth when He said to the Pharisees, "Your law says . . ."*
> *He did not say, "My law . . .' or 'God's law . . .*

Jesus presented love as the first and only requirement needed to fulfill the law of God. His message was an unbalanced portrayal of passionate love between God the Father and those He came to redeem.

Divine Union

Jesus' final night on Earth with His disciples was recorded by John in chapters 13-17. It is interesting to note that His parting words were not about the Law, keeping the Law, or any of the rabbinics which had become part of the Law. The key themes Jesus taught that night were love and joy. This is not just any love, but an exact representation of the love union between the Father and the Son. It was not just any joy, but a *fullness* of joy that is complete. The full concept of this should stop you in your tracks and carry you away at such thoughts. The message in these chapters is a non-status quo, an anti-status-quo. This mindset breaks the mold.

Consider the depth of the union we have been joined to:

> *I give you a new command: love one another.*[22] *As I have loved you, so you must love one another.*[23] *By this all people will know that you are my disciples, if you have love for one another.*[24] *As the Father has loved Me, I have also loved you. Remain in My love.*[25]

> *I have told you this so that my joy may be in you and that your joy may be complete.*[26] *Your grief will turn to joy.*[27] *You will rejoice and no one will take away your joy.*[28] *So that your joy may be full.*[29]

In this contemplation of love and joy, the Bible itself jumps off into deep space. It is like a free-fall into dangerous territory according to some, and a sweet love letter to others. Solomon's Song of Songs portrays a marriage patterned after divine love. Both Jewish and Christian biblical scholars have compared this book to the love of God for His people. The New Testament later tells us that a man's love for his wife should emulate Christ's love for His bride.[30] Paul's exhortation to the Corinthians explains this relationship further:

---

[22] Jn. 13:34.
[23] V. 34.
[24] Vs. 34-35.
[25] 15:9.
[26] V. 11.
[27] 16:20b.
[28] V. 22.
[29] V. 24 (NKJV).
[30] Eph. 5:22-23.

For I am jealous over you with a godly jealousy,
because I have promised you in marriage to one
husband—to present a pure virgin to Christ. (2
Corinthians 11:2, HCSB)

At the Last Supper, Jesus expounded on the law of love, an invitation to be swept into the Divine union of Father, Son, and Holy Spirit as one. This alone—the desire of God's passion for us—should leave us breathless.

Passionate Desire

Love has many hats, and the Lover of our souls wears them all. You may see yourself as a son on his Father's lap, or a general under the command of the host of Heaven, or the best friend of God, or His bride at the wedding supper of the Lamb. Whatever it is, it will be the most intimate relationship you have ever known.

This love relationship with our God is deep communion and intimate union with our Creator. This spirit-to-spirit communication allows for a continual flow where we don't have to wait until we die and "go to Heaven" to experience supernatural union. No, we can experience deep fellowship with Him right here on Earth, anywhere, anytime, because it is for this purpose we were created. And, He rewards those who earnestly run after Him.

You shall hide them in the secret place of Your
presence . . . (Psalm 31:20, NKJV)

The original Hebrew words for "Your presence" is "Your face." So it actually reads: "You shall hide them in the secret place of Your face . . ." I don't think the translators had a reference point to comprehend this. But to me, it is a more accurate picture of the intimate friendship God so desires with each of us. Since my heavenly vision, He has moved me moment by moment into a deeper, more passionate expression of love exchanged in our communion fueled by His desire. I am often overcome by the power of God's love to draw me into the secret place of His presence, His face.

The prophet Isaiah spoke about his passion for God and how he desired Him in the night seasons.

> *I long for You in the night; yes, my spirit within me diligently seeks You . . .* (Isaiah 26:9, HCSB)

The Hebrew word used here for "long for" is from the root word *avah*. It is the same word that was used for those who "lusted" after meat in the wilderness and God responded by sending them quail. In context, this verb is a passionate and longing cry of the heart for something that you have known before but are now missing. It is the kind of longing where you are fervently desiring it once again.

There just is no substitute for what God is stimulating you to desire with such deep longing. It is He, and He alone, who comes to that sanctuary created by Him and for Him, that secret place that dwells in the depths of your spirit. His presence will satisfy you there with a face-to-face encounter.

C. S. Lewis spoke truthfully when he said:

> *If I discover within myself a desire which no experience in this world can satisfy, the most probable explanation is that I was made for another world.*[31]

---

[31] Lewis, C.S. *Mere Christianity*, HarperCollins Publishers, 2001.

Furious Love

One of God's most intriguing names is "Jealous." It is a powerful view of God's furious love.

> Do not worship any other god, for the LORD, whose name is Jealous, is a jealous God. (Exodus 34:14)

In Solomon's Song, an analogy of love brings the book to an apex before it closes and reveals a jewel of God's heart.

> Set me as a seal on your heart, as a seal on your arm; for love is as strong as death; jealousy as cruel as the grave. Its flames are flames of fire, a most **vehement flame**. (8:6, NKJV, emphasis mine)

The term "vehement flame" is a single usage word in Scripture. It is the Hebrew word *shalhevet* which is the word for "flame." This word is used in two other Scriptures. However, here in this passage, it is a compound word with God's name, "Yah," attached to it, *shalhevet-Yah*. God attaches His own name to a characteristic that links us together in deep, intimate union with Him as "an unquenchable flame of passionate love."

The best way to describe the intensity of this flame is that of white phosphorous. Once ignited, white phosphorous cannot be extinguished. You can throw it in water and it will lick up the water like gasoline. Until the source is utterly exhausted, it is a blazing furious inferno. This is the description God gives about His passion for us, and I am compelled to respond to such love.

This word is also used in Ezekiel in a prophecy against the Negev forest, now a very dry and desolate desert.

*Say to the southern forest: "Hear the word of the LORD. This is what the Sovereign LORD says: 'I am about to set fire to you and it will consume all your trees, both green and dry. The blazing **flame** will not be quenched, and every face from south to north will be scorched by it.'"* (Ezekiel 20:47, emphasis mine)

The word "flame" is again *shalhevet*, but it does not have God's name attached to it. The point is intensity.

As we consider the desire of God with a jealous, intense, furious passion that burns hot like white phosphorus, a whole new understanding opens to us in regards to the intimacy He longs for. In this place of passionate communion with God, there are no restrictions or limits.

He is wooing you from the jaws of distress to a spacious place free from restriction, to the comfort of your table laden with choice food. (Job 36:16)

God's furious love is continually drawing us into a deeper, more intimate, and satisfying relationship with Him. He is not narcissistic, in need of mindless worshipers for the sake of being worshiped. Rather, this is a love story with two intimate partners who simply cannot get enough of each other and continually seek to burn with this unquenchable fiery love. With each day, I am pressing more into Him, releasing more of myself in surrender to His passion, and I do not allow anything to hinder our relationship.

Created to Love Passionately

God created us with the capacity to love Him and be loved extravagantly by Him. He created us body, soul, and spirit to enjoy intimate union and constant communion with Him.

The beloved Body of Christ has been under an oppressive identity crisis for centuries, wherein we have been lied to, disabling us so that we are unable to love or be loved by the very One who desires us the most. With these lies has come a mindset of degrading self-abasement which steals Heaven's perspective of us and our rightful authority given through the blood of Jesus. The evil realm of darkness seeks to undermine and accuse us continually with lying whispers about that which has already been dealt with by His blood. We have bought in to putting on a false humility instead of appropriating the finished work Jesus did on the cross. The fact is, Jesus has dealt with our accuser and his lies of shame once and for all.

> *The accuser of our brothers has been thrown out: the one who accuses them before our God day and night.* (Revelation 12:10)

The best way to war against the enemy who tries to accuse you of your past is to speak out what Jesus has provided for you in your present and future through His blood, and then worship Him with thanksgiving. The enemy will not stay around for a love exchange between you and God. You only need remember why you were created—to love God passionately with everything in you—and then do just that. Your accuser will be instantly silenced.

Never Forsaken

We have a beautiful assurance from Scripture that God will never leave us or forsake us—though everyone else in our life may do that, He never will. God told this to the Israelites again and again.

> *He who appoints the sun to shine by day, who decrees the moon and stars to shine by night, who stirs up the sea so that its waves roar—the LORD Almighty is his name: Only if these decrees vanish from my sight, declares the LORD, will the descendants of Israel ever cease to be a nation before me."* (Jeremiah 31:35-36)

God has never forsaken His people Israel, and Carol and I are testimonies to this fact of His ongoing goodness to them. Before He ascended, Jesus assured His disciples of His continual presence with them by promising to send the Holy Spirit. In the same way, I believe the Father, Son, and Holy Spirit experience continual union without any separation. Even when Jesus carried our sins on the cross, I do not believe their union was interrupted by God turning away. How could God turn His back on His only Son at the moment when the universe was split, the plan of the ages was accomplished, the very plan that was in existence from the foundation of the earth?

As I have studied Psalm 22, I see a very different picture of that moment. From the cross, Jesus quotes the first line of this Psalm aloud:

> *My God, my God, why have You forsaken me . . . But I am a worm and not a man, scorned by men and despised by people. Everyone who sees me mocks me; they sneer and shake their heads: "He relies on the LORD; let Him rescue him; let the LORD deliver him, since He takes pleasure in him."* (Psalm 22:1, 6-8)

I would like to focus on two points in this Psalm that I believe have been misunderstood. The first one is that God forsook Jesus because of the weight of our sin. The second is that we are lowly and worthless as worms.

A background understanding and context for this is much more interesting and liberating for His beloved bride. Remember, no one had a compact Bible in the time of Jesus, and therefore, the common people memorized large portions of Scripture by singing them so they could quote or chant these with the synagogue leaders. The writings and Law of Moses were written on large scrolls kept in the synagogues and were read only on Shabbat.[32] It was customary for one person to begin a Psalm by chanting the first line, and soon others would join in with the remainder of the Psalm, much the same way we would start the first line of a song. In this context let's consider what may have really happened when Jesus shouted out the first line of Psalm 22 from the cross:

> *About three in the afternoon, Jesus cried out with a loud voice . . ." My God, my God, why have You forsaken Me?"* (Matthew 27:45, NKJV)

First of all, why did Jesus cry out with a loud voice? Could God not hear a whisper? I believe it was so He could be heard by the those at the foot of the cross, knowing full well the people would recite by memory the remaining Psalm. The rest of the Psalm is now playing like a recording in the hearts and minds of those watching.

This brings us to the place of the second misunderstanding.

> *I am a worm and not a man.* (v. 6)

Incorrectly we have assumed that the word "worm" refers to our lowly position before God. The theology of the degradation of the believer is now set in stone. Or is it? The Hebrew word for "worm" is *to'alat*. In my research on this word, it presented what I believe is a proper understanding of what Jesus was

---

[32] *Shabbat* is the Hebrew word for "Sabbath."

communicating from the cross. Coccus ilicis, is a worm from whose body comes the ancient world's scarlet color and crimson dye. This worm would climb a special oak tree which only grows in the Mediterranean region. Then the worm attaches its head in the bark permanently. Once attached, the worm then lays its eggs under its body, covers them with a scarlet secretion, wraps its body gently around them in the shape of a human heart, turns white, and dies.

This worm was harvested by first century Jewish priests to squeeze the scarlet from the heart-shape and use the dye to color the sashes of the priests who performed the sin offerings in the temple. The dye was colorfast and brilliant.

When Psalm 22 was proclaimed aloud by the Messiah as His bloodied body hung on that cross, and all the crowd immediately recited its prophetic passages by heart, the *to'alat* worm and its purpose was unveiled. Jesus' eternal act was permanent, His atonement brilliant, and the unmistakable power of God was immediately manifested: rocks split, the sky turned stormy black, the veil of the temple was torn in half, and tombs were opened as many witnessed deceased saints wandering the city of Jerusalem.

That kind of manifestation of the power of Heaven does not happen when God turns His back. God had not forsaken His people, but rather, declared with vivid proof the provision of eternal redemption with His very presence.

Treasured by the Father

The liberating message is that, as God's beloved ones, we are treasured. He does not turn away from us in displeasure when we fail. Jesus' blood cleanses us from all sin. In fact, He is there to take us to a new place, where all appetite for sin gets washed away and displaced by something so much more delicious. Nothing compares to this glorious union.

The injunction of Jesus, "go and sin no more," was not a threat; rather, it was an inoculation against the magnetic drawing power of sin. There will be no more skulking away from God's presence when we fail—allowing a little time to go by so He can look at us again. Intimacy can only be cultivated to the degree that we feel we are unconditionally loved and treasured. We have been lied to for too long; God is restoring the identity of the bride He is passionate about. Jesus is not returning for a pitiful, whining, victimized bridal partner. No, His bride is a victorious, combat boot-stomping, destroyer of satan's evil works, and she is in love with her Bridegroom.

The gears of the universe are oiled by intimacy. Guilt and shame cloud the soul and spirit. Whereas, the fresh revelation that we are loved and accepted brings clarity to confused and tormented minds.

Paul had a clear understanding of his authority and position before God and was able to speak boldly on His behalf even when things turned ugly against him. For instance, as be begins to make his speech standing before the council of the Sanhedrin, he is promptly struck in the face. Angry, Paul yells out:

> *God is going to strike you, you whitewashed wall!*
> *You are sitting there judging me according to the*
> *law, and in violation of the law are you ordering me*
> *to be struck?* (Acts 23:3)

The bystanders announced to Paul that he was speaking to the high priest! Paul did not miss a beat. He apologized, responding in an instant because he was confident about his identity as beloved in Christ. He then succeeds in turning the focus off himself by throwing the controversial issue of the resurrection between the Pharisees and the Sadducees. The discussion became violent, not toward Paul, but toward each other, so that he had to be rescued from the ensuing fray. Clear-minded thinking only comes from a spirit yoked to the fire of

God in the strength of intimacy.

Because we are engaged in an ongoing spiritual war, we must know that intimate friendship with God is the most valuable weapon at our disposal, but we need to know how it works.

Passion for God

First and foremost, crazy faith is about passionate love for God. I can only contrast anemic and lukewarm love with the true, passionate, and fiery first-love that Jesus desires by my own mindset and personal experience. To accuse others of having my previous mindset would be unfair. However, as I describe the contrast of my previous relationship with Jesus and where I am now, it draws out a fair majority of Christians who have admitted that they have settled for what they realize is an anemic, passive, lukewarm, religiously-active and works-driven relationship. I have observed that people around the world are simply starving for a genuine, vibrant relationship with Jesus— as I was—and they admit they have lived too long dissatisfied, bored, and restless.

The spirit of a man bypasses intellect and clings to a heart that is ablaze with passion.

King David provoked an unusual demonstration of God's love in Psalm 18. The provocation was itself an unusual declaration of his own love for God.

I love You, LORD, my strength. (v.1)

The ancient Hebrew word for "love" that David uses is a single-usage word in Scripture, *erchamcha-na*. The same word is also used in a beautiful song called "El Shaddai,"[33] made

---

[33] "El Shaddai," written by Michael Card and John Thompson,

popular by Christian singer Amy Grant in the 80s. Many people have asked me about the Hebrew word she used in the song that says, "El Shaddai, El Shaddai, **erchamcha**-na Adonai."

The root of the Hebrew word *erchamcha* can mean "mercy," but it is also the root word for "womb." With this understanding, David's proclamation here describes him as so wrapped in the security of God's love, he compares it to being in utero (unborn)—in complete safety with God's enveloping, protective love.

God's Passion for Us

God's response to David assures him with descriptive imagery that not only was His nurturing love with him in the distressing situation, but all the forces of Heaven were coming to his defense as well. In fact, the same Psalm portrays a vivid scene of how God Himself would take action.

> *He rode on a cherub and flew, soaring on the wings of the wind.* (v. 10)

The Hebrew word *cherub* has often been pictured as chubby little angel children with teeny wings. *Cheruv*, however, was creatively depicted by the ancient Hebrew artists as resembling Brahma bulls with wings. These strong, giant creatures, their bodies covered in eyes, were to be feared. There are many other images in Scripture of *cheruv'im*[34] that suggest to us that they are created heavenly beasts with very specific roles.

In defense of David, who was terribly stressed by his enemies at the writing of this Psalm, he sees God saddling up a *cheruv* and riding the winds to save the day, dragging storm clouds down all around Him. The recorded effects in Psalm 18 are stunning.

Myrrh Records, 1982.

[34] The plural form of *cheruv* is *cheruv'im*.

He rode on a cherub and flew, soaring on the wings of the wind. He made darkness His hiding place, dark storm clouds His canopy around Him. From the radiance of His presence, His clouds swept onward with hail and blazing coals. The LORD thundered from heaven; the Most High projected His voice. He shot His arrows and scattered them; He hurled lightning bolts and routed them (18:10-19).

I see God responding with His fierce, fiery, jealous passion on behalf of David—His beloved!—in distress yet fully trusting His full deliverance.

I spoke in a rural Oklahoma church and made mention of this section of Scripture. Suddenly you could pick out every cowboy in the congregation. They sat up square in their pews, eyes bright and excited, and they almost could not contain themselves waiting to speak to me after the service. These Oklahoma cowboys spent the next day trying to rustle up a Brahma bull for me to ride just to show their appreciation for validating their unique and often misunderstood lives direct from the pages of the Bible. The picture for these cowboys of seeing God rescue his beloved one riding a bull-cherub was much more plausible than mounting a little chubby baby-cherub.

I was pretty relieved, actually, that they didn't find that bull for me to ride.

Yoked to the Fire

My awakening vision opened doors to the fire room of His Majesty. His love-on-fire is stronger than anything I have yet to encounter and I have yoked myself to that fire.

Jesus was presented with a question about which of the 613 commandments was the greatest. His answer, I believe, revealed the fire of His heart: a passionate, all-out, surrendered love for

God—heart, soul, mind[35]—the kind of love that gives with all you have! Jesus' conversation with His disciples about love on their last night together must be combined with this answer to get the full meaning of what He is looking for. As Jesus and His disciples celebrated the Passover meal together, He imparted deep truths and important tenets of the Kingdom, fully expecting that His impartation would powerfully transform their lives.

Some would say that Jesus was modeling humility by washing the disciples' feet at the Passover table. I believe His act was only a small part of what was really going on. The fact is, Jesus was in love! He loved His intimate friends with the same passion He shared with God the Father. That concept takes some meditation to really grasp and accept. To crave contact with the object of love is natural. Washing each one of His disciples feet individually was more than an example of servanthood; it was an intimate exchange and demonstration of His fiery love and passion. He knew they would respond to His love with their lives, and likewise, love one another as He patterned.

On this night before He was betrayed, Jesus emphasized love for one another as He loved with celebrative joy despite persecution. Being yoked together with joy in the fire of His love would be a stronghold for them against the approaching storm. The brilliant commands Jesus unfolded to them eclipsed the demands of the Law and could only be carried out by the "new" man. The path to that new man was hinted at: "the Comforter" would come. No further explanation was needed: the coming Spirit of Truth, the Counselor, would take care of everything.

The Holy Spirit enjoins us to cultivate the kind of love for one another that is so outwardly demonstrative that outsiders take notice. Hearts are easily knit together and strengthened as we gather together to share God's goodness, and as we do,

---

[35]   Matt. 22:35-37.

God Himself leans in to our conversations as we delight in His goodness.

> *Then they that feared the LORD spake often one to another: and the LORD hearkened, and heard it; and a book of remembrance was written before him for them that feared the LORD, and that thought upon his name."* (Malachi 3:16, KJV)

It seems that God is so moved by our conversations about Him that He keeps a heavenly scrapbook. He takes notice and calls for the heavenly scribe to record in detail when we gather to revel in His goodness. He celebrates our love on fire for Him and our love for one another.

Crazy in Love

I have realized that I have fallen in love with Jesus again—crazy in love. It has reordered my core values and future plans. My body, soul, mind, and spirit are preoccupied with the pleasure of His companionship. I find that my every waking moment seeks to let Him fill me to overflowing and then spill out through me to everyone.

I have observed that abandonment to love radically changed my world view and rearranged my priorities. What was important before does not hold the same value as it once did. Terminally ill patients say this is what happens when facing possible death. At the end of their life, people become much more relationship-focused and God-focused.

The Shulamite, the beloved one of the king in the Song of Songs, refers many times to her state as being "lovesick." Her focus, now that she is lovesick, is no longer on the vineyard or tending her flock, but rather, on the object of her love. In her lovesickness, her values become His values; her desires switch away from the mundane to the heights as her heart is caught away in the rapture of love, much like a gazelle bounding on the mountaintops. Her focus has been lifted above the daily tasks to the lofty otherworldly "real" world of eternity. She becomes the focus of those around her who see her passion as attractive.

God is drawn to those who are passionate towards Him. The majority of His Book centers around those with their love abandoned to that crazy state of lovesickness. This state is not too dissimilar to a teenager's first love experience, where desire for food becomes secondary, staring with that dazed, far-away look, contented to dream about the object of his affection, while ignoring the cares of everyday life.

Jesus' injunction in the book of Revelation is His pleading to return to our "first love."

> *Nevertheless, I have somewhat against you because you have left your first love.* (Revelation 2:4)

I admit it. I am crazy in love with Jesus and have been caught engaged in all of the above listed as lovesickness. I declare Him to be the object of all my affections, and I have returned happily to my first love. His affection toward me is the rarified atmosphere of Heaven that causes me to soar to the heights and leads me into a place of deep adoration.

Devotion in Adoration

The invasion of Heaven into my life in my "awakening" was nuclear. The landscape was bombed out, made desolate, and in smoldering ruins for a short time. The foundations of my spiritual life were bulldozed. Jesus' goal was not desolation, but rather, an infusion of the abundant life which I had been missing. His life obliterated the pitiful debris I had traded for the treasures of Heaven.

The shame of my previous lukewarm state, with guilt-driven devotions, and list after list of personal wants and needs became overwhelming. One day I pondered, *Had I ever once asked Him, "What do You want . . . what do You need?"* I determined that what He really wanted from me was the rest of my life spent in adoration. It was in this posture, rightly aligned with Him, that I discovered all of my prayers were being answered.

The glory of His Majesty eclipses everything. I am pretty sure that John the beloved, while on the Isle of Patmos, never thought up a prayer list, he could barely breathe at the sight of the resurrected, glorified Jesus. Daniel, in the presence of the messenger angel, fell down dead on the spot and had to be touched and revived awake. The priests in the temple, when the glory of the Lord descended could not even stand up, let alone perform their duties.

Jesus the Bridegroom has longed for this same passionate response to be awakened in His Bride. He is ravished by her.

> *Turn your eyes away from me for they captivate me.*
> (Song of Songs 6:5)

He has waited for our affection and adoration and is finally now receiving what He has longed for. Jesus' wants and needs are you, and He wants you every hour of every day.

Eternal Adoration

What is adoration? It is "fervent and devoted love" given with "deep affection." There is a place in worship where our posture is not the focus, the songs we sing don't seem quite appropriate, there is no form to the worship expression, we find no words to tell Jesus, and all we can do is stare in awe and wonder at His beauty. From deep within comes a vocabulary of love, spirit expressions that are a wordless exchange of our heart to His and His heart to us. In this place there are no needs, no requests—we are only loving Him and declaring our trust solely in Him.

As we behold Him, His beauty is all we see, and that is what we declare back to Him. In beholding Him, we are transported into His presence where nothing and no one can intrude this secret place. It is in this place of adoration we become "lost," where we are completely unaware of people around us and where we even lose track of time.

I (Carol) have been lost in this place, at times, for hours. I often will go into that deep place of adoration of the Lord when I have retired for the evening. Perhaps because it is quiet and I can be assured there will be no distractions or interruptions that will make demands on me. I am completely relaxed and focused on giving love to the Lover of my soul. Also, if I am distressed about something and finding it difficult to process, I intentionally enter into adoration knowing I will find God's peace and affirmation of love. While I am adoring the Lord, I am not striving for answers or direction—just communing with Him.

Adoration often begins with thanksgiving and praise for all He has done as I reflect on the day, current situations, and the concerns of my heart. In this place, I release them all to God's care. From there, I enter into a time of worship, just adoring Jesus and who He is in eternity. The Holy Spirit is the One who leads me. He is, after all, my worship leader.

What I have discovered in this place of deep adoration is the power of our intimacy released as I am adoring Jesus. There have been times when my body has been wracked with pain and I find no natural or medicinal relief. It is in these times of deep adoration that I discover relief from pain. In fact, God has often healed my painful condition completely as I am adoring Him. I find that amazing. I also believe that, as I am adoring the

Lord in a corporate setting, God is releasing His healing power over people who need healing in their bodies and souls through my adoration of Him. As I sing before His presence, adoring Him, the power of the Lord is present to heal. Because of this, I often sing over people, and they experience healing in their bodies and souls. As I have sung over people, adoring Jesus, I have received testimonies of healing from migraine headaches, diabetes, depression, joint pain, grief, and more.

I encourage you to go deeper in worship with a more focused time of adoration. The next time your body needs relief from pain or you are distressed with life issues, enter into that deep place of worship and then transition into a time of simply adoring Jesus. Get lost in His presence; and in the love exchange, you will experience a healing transformation of body and soul and be strengthened deep in your spirit.

Stoking the Fire

Fresh, surprise encounters will keep our love for Jesus hot and fiery. Such intimacy with Jesus keeps all erroneous motives and other competing affections at bay. There are ways to stoke the fire of seeing clearly how Heaven sees you. Very soon you will find that the fire burns of its own accord and out of control. What does stoking the fire look like?

I (Ron) was driving across Wyoming . . . grass, grass, grass, one inch tall from horizon to horizon for hundreds of miles. Normally, this could be extremely boring. God laughs and whispers to me: "I made every blade of that grass for you—specifically for you! Just think about that! Put just one blade under an electron microscope and you will see a universe of wonder. I have every blade counted and assigned to its task. Many of them no one will ever see, yet I know them all."

I know how God views stars and has the hairs on my head counted, but blades of grass? In response, I had to pull my car over to the side of the road and get out to keep from driving into a ditch, I was so overcome.

Think about this: Every atom, every molecule, every quark[36] was created to bring you pleasure forever more. Everything is for you. Everything! God's fire is so passionate, I think it would dismember you if He did not burn His love in a controlled manner. He searches the earth for those wholly committed to this love relationship with Him so He can stoke the fires.

> For the eyes of the LORD range throughout the earth to strengthen those whose hearts are fully committed to him. (2 Chronicles 16:9, NIV)

Encountering and releasing God's fiery passion—being zealous for His heart, His ways, His people—will compel us to right the injustice perpetrated by the kingdom of darkness upon nations, people groups, widows and orphans, etc. His love and compassion will be the fuel that propels us further than we ever thought possible, to go to places we could not have imagined, all because we are navigated by love so powerful, it transforms the darkest environments.

Love will cause us to lay down everything and give up all to pursue the one passion of God's heart—manifesting His love and compassion to every person, no matter the personal cost. That is the driving force behind Jesus' final words to His disciples: *Go! Just go! I'll be with you always . . . go into every corner of the earth . . . tell them. Will you please tell them I love them?*

---

[36] Subatomic building blocks of matter.

That moment
when you just know
God is about to do
something
extraordinary . . .

THE GREAT EXCHANGE

A fool hath no delight in understanding, but that his heart may discover itself. (Proverbs 18:2, KJV)

A few weeks before finding Christ, I (Ron) located a secluded moonlit spot between the pilings of the Venice Beach pier. Darkness fenced me in on three sides, and waves pounded the shore behind me. Very carefully, I drew a large pentagram in the sand with my heel, and then etched a circle around it. I followed the directives from the book on witchcraft with precision. With the symbols drawn in the sand, I stepped into the pentagram and demanded power from the unseen realm. I was absolutely unprepared for what happened next. I'm not sure what I expected, but raw reality stunned me.

Trading my Soul?

Suddenly, a dark voice from the blackness directly in front of me answered, "I'll give you power . . . but, in exchange, I want your soul!"

My blood froze. I had read Faust and knew what it meant to sell your soul to the devil. I had come unprepared for this demand for the transaction of the eternal possession of my soul. I was just looking for some power. I stood frozen as I considered this, wondering just how deep I had already gotten myself into this realm.

Behind me another voice, calm, yet strong, asked a question: "Where do you know satan from?"

Hearing the voice so audibly that it spun me around, I was just sure someone had come up behind me. But only the ocean waves crashed upon the shore in the moonlit night behind me. I peered into the deep darkness. No one was there.

I turned again to face my dilemma. *Could I just step out of this pentagram and go home?* I wondered. The voice behind me spoke again, this time more resolute, as if I had not heard.

"Where do you know satan from?"

I turned my head once again, just to make sure that no one was behind me, but all I saw was moonlight dancing on the waves.

What? My mind queried the star-studded night sky with a restless unease. There was no pause. I was summoned again in answer to my bewilderment at being interrogated by the unseen.

"Where do you know satan from?"

Now my mind was reeling. Warring voices were competing for my attention. I sensed the dark voice had been silenced by my invisible examiner as the question hung thickly in the air demanding an immediate answer.

"Well," I responded, my eyes scanning the horizon, "from the Bible."

"So, why would you join the losing team?" came the calm, authoritative reply. With the reality of this truth came an overwhelming, otherworldly peace. I discovered later that this is Heaven's clear thinking and calming atmosphere. I threw the book of witchcraft into the crashing ocean waves and walked home.

Just a few weeks later, a midnight fire destroyed the Aragon Ballroom on the Lick Pier at Venice Beach, California, while thousands watched. At one point, offshore winds bore leaping embers 1,000-feet onto nearby buildings. The scene of the war for my soul had become a blazing inferno, and only years later was I able to conclude that the enemy lost the bargain that night and was enraged.

California Trippin'

Over the years of my running from the unseen Voice, I had become a habitual drug user and stopped counting my LSD trips because they were so numerous. I remember calculating one day whether I could actually afford to be a heroin user, but concluded I could not. My need for spiritual experiences was intensifying, and the enemy of my soul was right there to recommend the very next thing I craved. I sought out risky and dangerous company, hanging around Hollywood's Sunset Strip in southern California for the next thrill-seeking moment.

My escapades during these crazy years would lead me further and deeper into every kind of pleasure-seeking activity and more intense spiritual experiences, all the while attempting to satisfy an unquenchable desire of my soul.

Hippie Haven

In 1969, I traveled to San Francisco with a van full of friends wanting to hang out with the Haight-Ashbury hippies. We wound up one day at the hippie commune deep in the Mendocino woods of northern California. Here, millionaire Sabine Ball purchased acreage and welcomed hundreds of hippies to her commune. It was a free-thinking, anything-goes utopia of free drugs, free sex, and free for all.

There, on the steps of Sabine's cabin in the woods sat a hippie reading a book.

"Hey man," I asked, "what are you reading?" As it turned out, he was reading *The Imitation of Christ*.[37] All the while, the plans of the unbodied Voice unfolded, hemming me in with a perfect "unperturbed pace," chasing me down and getting closer.

A year after this incident I learned that my beloved eldest sister Betty and her three daughters had received Christ. Just the thought of this made my skin crawl and shook my world. I had worked long and hard to silence the Voice in my head that shed light on my sins. The news of their conversion opened up a can of worms. The Voice was wooing me. . .silent, but wooing me.

I was proud to have been initiated into Transcendental Meditation at UCLA by Maharishi Mahesh Yogi, also the spiritual leader of John Lennon of The Beatles. My religion was no dumbed-down pie-in-the-sky. No siree. I was considered part of the spiritual upper-crust. *Besides that* (inwardly defending my case), *Paramahansa Yogananda*[38] *wrote that Jesus Himself taught you had to be reincarnated.*[39]

---

[37] Kempis, Thomas à. *The Imitation of Christ*.

[38] Yogananda, Paramahansa. *Autobiography of a Yogi*. Copyright 1946.

[39] Yoganada, based his argument on John chapter 3.

The unbodied Voice was closing in. My mansion of cards was about to come crashing down. The revelation unveiled over the next couple of days had me in a fury. Somewhere I located a New Testament, opened to John chapter three to settle once and for all this unpalatable Christian dogma. As I read the chapter, however, my heart sank. *Paramahansa could not have been more wrong,* I realized. *Reincarnation is not here at all!* The message of Jesus was rebirth by the Spirit, plain and simple.

The Voice came back in force, and I struggled to silence it. Even though it had saved me from satan's grip on my soul that night on the beach under the pier, I was unprepared to give all for what I did not intellectually understand.

Sign From Heaven

Following this close call with the truth revealed in John's Gospel, I decided to ask God Himself. *After all,* I reasoned, *I'm a card-carrying follower of a well-known Yogi. I have spirituality...*

"God, if what I read is really You, give me a sign." That was it.

The very next day, sitting on the beach in Venice and enjoying the quiet, a friend and I were playing the Japanese board game called Go. Out of nowhere, the warm sun was blocked by a wall of bodies surrounding our blanket. My friend just seemed to evaporate while I sat there stunned at this crowd of 400 appearing so suddenly and trying to figure out why they were there.

Still puzzling over this, I hustled to pick up my belongings to make a quick exit when a young man plopped down on my beach blanket. With a big grin and starry eyes, he looked directly at me and crooned, "Do you know how much Jesus loves you?"

I was shocked, and then outraged. *This can't be happening.*

"What is this?" I asked with a sweep of my hand toward the large crowd surrounding us.

"Oh, this is our church baptism!" he answered eagerly.

"In Venice Beach?" I snapped back sarcastically. "Listen, they kill people here!" I added for dramatic effect, gathering up my scattered game pieces.

Undeterred, the young man stretched out on my blanket and began sharing about Jesus and the Bible. Quickly stuffing the last of the items into my bag, I shot back, "Listen, I read somewhere that you can measure your Christian Heaven with a measuring stick," pausing for effect. "That means there couldn't possibly be room for everyone." With that I snatched my beach blanket he was still sitting on and headed through the crowd of "happy people" who had invaded my little safe spot.

But inside. . . Inside I knew God had answered my inquiry. . .this was indeed the sign I had asked Him for.

The unbodied Voice smirked.

I smoldered.

The fence moved in closer.

Jesus People

The following week, out of the blue, my sister Betty called and invited me to a birthday party—my birthday party. The hippie lifestyle I was living had caused her to forbid me from seeing my teenage nieces, Terri, Connie, and Kathy, and I had missed them terribly.

"I have to warn you, however," she said, "the whole family has received Jesus and things are very different in our home now." I cringed inside at the thought of this, but I was also really excited for the chance to be with them. I had spent much time growing up in their home over the years, and religious differences aside, I was looking forward to some family time.

When I arrived, Bibles were drawn out like pistols, pages

flipped like a windstorm, fingers wagged at me, and sin accusations were thrown my direction like firebrands. I remained calm through it all, maintaining my air of spiritual superiority knowing I had been initiated into the very elite, high order of religious practice.

"Well," I promised them all, "I'll meet you up there," pointing toward Heaven. I quelled their nagging anxiety about my eternal destiny with a few clever quips from gurus. My nieces did not have the answers to my intellectual religious ranting. They retreated in defeat and momentary discouragement.

Bounding back a few moments later with renewed courage, my niece Connie boldly announced, "Promise you'll go with us to the Jesus People coffee house tonight, Uncle Ronnie!"

Oh no! I thought. I gave every excuse I could muster to get out of it. None worked. I was stuck. It was, after all, *my* birthday and I was obligated to celebrate with them.

I suddenly had a plan. *I'll just show up there and act like everyone else and no one will be the wiser that sin entered their camp.* I carefully plotted to arrive at the coffee house and sit near the back so I could slip out unnoticed in case things got too hot.

The unbodied Voice smirked, but I was unaware.

We arrived and soon discovered that Connie had pre-arranged where the family would sit. She dragged me right up to sit with them all in the front. I acquiesced because I love her. The fact is, I would do anything my nieces asked of me.

The coffee house floor was lined with carpet sample squares, and everyone sat on the floor. *Just act like everyone else. Stay cool. This will be over soon*, I assured myself.

The first half of the meeting was a music concert with a fairly good band. I was actually surprised this Christian group performing could play such good contemporary music as I was expecting an old fashioned, Gospel quartet with accordions.

Unnoticed by me, some of my defenses fell.

At the half-time break, everyone stood and wrapped their arms around the person's shoulders next to them and they began to sing the Lord's Prayer.

Aha! I thought. *I know the words to this song.* I figured no one had caught on to the fact that I was just playing along, an imposter in their midst. Swaying back and forth, singing Jesus' words with a hundred teenagers was so different than mindlessly chanting a mantra of Eastern meditation's cold and impersonal approach to satisfy spiritual hunger.

More defenses fell, again, unnoticed by me.

Encountering Love

We came to the last line of the prayer singing acapella all together, "For Thine is the Kingdom, and the power, and the glory forever. . ." When suddenly, the unbodied Voice snatched me right out of the room into outer space. Total darkness surrounded me. And then, I heard that Voice. . . again . . .

"The words that are coming out of your mouth right now are Truth. Do you want to be part of that Kingdom?"

Suddenly, all my defenses came crashing down and I simply exploded in tears—wracking sobs is more like it. In that moment, I got it . . . all of my questions, concerns, and anxieties were satisfied at the sound of His voice. All I could do was cry uncontrollably as I basked in that otherworldly peace again.

What is happening to me? My mind could not reason it, but, at the same time, I could not stop crying. It seemed that once the flood gate was opened from inside of me, everything began to fall into place and instantly make sense. The reality of His Truth completely undid me. I actually do not know how long I was weeping before God's presence. I felt clean inside . . . so clean.

It was only later I learned that my family and their friends from the coffee house had been praying for me, some even fasting, for a week leading up to this night. God had really set me up. But even with the thorough washing of tears, He was not finished on this evening. There was more. Two bubble gum-chewing teens skipped up to me, tears still streaming down my face. "Come with us!" Then leading me by the hand into a back room they announced, "The Holy Spirit wants to give you a new prayer language!"

"You mean like this?" With that, I spontaneously began to praise God in a heavenly language. It felt like I was speaking directly to God. No English words came out of my mouth. My heart was exploding again and again from deep within me in praise for His incredible goodness.

At some point, I turned around and all I could do was grab my family and hug them. "Thank you!" There were a lot of joyful tears at this rebirth-day celebration of mine.

Later, as I recalled the events of that night, I considered that God brought no condemnation for my wild, sinful life. I felt no sense of impatience at how long it took me to "get it," nor did I receive harsh words for my rebelliousness in turning away from Him so intentionally all those years. All I felt was His love . . . pure love. It was, in fact, the very atmosphere of the Kingdom that I so glibly sang about in the Lord's Prayer as I pretended to fit in. In that moment of revelation, I had experienced the Truth in the Person of Jesus and encountered God's passion that had gone after me and won my heart affections.

As we left the coffee house that night, the world appeared crystal clear, as if newly cleansed. Colors I had never seen before sparkled like brilliant diamonds from the city lights. I was experiencing my world with new eyes that no drug could ever match. I was washed clean, a brand new person, and I knew that I now belonged to the King of the universe.

Satan had forever lost the battle for my soul.

The Crazy Journey Begins

The journey with the Holy Spirit and adventures in crazy faith had begun. I evacuated the city of Venice within a week knowing that to straddle the fence of my old life was more than dangerous, it would be spiritual suicide. I was baptized in water shortly thereafter in a small church, along with my nieces and my sister Betty.

Within a year, I enrolled in a short-term, intensive missionary training school where God unfolded His plan for my life. There I met my wonderful wife Carol. At the publishing of this book, we are celebrating 40 years together as husband and wife.

Saved, Satisfied, and Delivered

Sadly, I have spent many of my previous years in personal agony of soul as I dealt with issues of identity and self-worth. It was only after my awakening vision of the majesty of God in Heaven that I finally received full deliverance and freedom. From that moment on, I came to appreciate the person He made me to be. I learned to drink deep from the wells of His love where everything within me was fully satisfied. It is true that no one person on the face of this earth could ever satisfy the deepest longings we have. That has been reserved only for the Lover of our soul.

The key is to learn to take from Jesus everything we need to satisfy the craving deep within us. When I began to learn how to love God and to receive His extravagant love, I found I had no more cravings of my flesh and no longer needed to indulge in the substitutes the world offered. Learning to dwell in God's presence where full satisfaction is received is the key to maintaining the deliverance He provides. The only way to sustain personal revival is to drink deeply from the One who created you for His pleasure alone.

One night God told me, "Get paper and pen, and write." He immediately began to speak; I was writing so fast, I could hardly keep up. There was no time to ponder sentence structure and content; it was live-stream from Heaven.

"The Book of You" has overwhelmed me many times as I have reread it since that night. Many times, over the years, I have shared it with various friends, and whenever I do, I am always surprised to see that it has the same effect on them as it did me. As you read this, you may sense this is a prayer declaration for a loved one.

The fact is, Heaven has a much different idea about our former life prior to Jesus and the choices we made. When we come to the end of a self-made man or woman and see that our lifestyle is empty and destructive in and of itself, Heaven invades and creates a life-transformational encounter with God Himself. For it is He who actually wrote a different life-script for us, and when we are ready to embrace Him—fully surrendered—powerful changes in the depths of our being deliver us from the hell-hole of addictions and destruction into a wellspring of life. Though the changes He makes in us are deeply personal, we are empowered to impart that same freedom to others.

So, I would like to share "The Book of You" here, and I pray that you will hear God speak tenderly to your own heart. May He remind you of the person you truly are—the one He created you to be, your God-given identity. May it overwhelm and transform everything else that seeks to choke out the truth. May this be a declaration that transforms you and draws you into that secret place where you offer Him a surrendered heart full of gratitude and worship. May you see the One who loves you. Amen.

The Book of You

I LOOKED on you in great love before you were formed in the womb (Ps. 139:15). I saw the number of your days and the day of your turning away from Me.

IN PATIENCE, I waited for you. My Father's heart yearned for you—yearned for your wholeness, the wholeness I had already written in My "book-of-you" (v. 16).

I SAW the chains you chose above My jewels. I watched the bonds you forged take you far away; but, I knew and I waited. I knew you had My justice deep in your heart. I saw you cry out, and I loved what I saw. I loved your heart, though chained and dark. I knew you would come through because, I had written it in My "book-of-you."

EVEN IN chains, you loved holiness. Even in chains, you cried for My purity.

THE DAY dawned; I danced (Zeph. 3:17). I sang the longed-for song, the song I wrote in My "book-of-you." I sang the song; I took your chains and forged a crown that will be yours forever. I took cold iron, and I made gold.

HEAVEN gasped at My deed.

THEY SPOKE your new name fresh on their lips; first like a whisper in the trees, then like rushing water. They spoke the name I wrote in the book. Then they shouted it.

THE DAY dawned, the book now sheds its mighty power over you. Heaven's genetics now crowd out Earth's.

MY NURTURING heart will now nourish you—strengthening you to step into the fullness of whom I wrote.

THE CROWN will be your testimony for your days down there, but here—near My throne—it radiates glory, healing virtue, strength of character, right character—My character—My law of you, written before you were formed.

BEHOLD the person I made. Love the person I made as I love.

PATIENTLY I waited until you laid down your will; that strong seed of Me that makes you like unto Me. I placed that surrendered will as the crown jewel in your crown to bear witness to all Heaven, for eternity, of the victory over what you thought an unchangeable, immutable character flaw.

FORGIVE "YOU" now as I do. Don't avoid you. Look straight into your own eyes and love you as I do.

Your vision must see
so far above and
beyond where
you are presently so that
everything you do
functions
as the heartbeat
towards that.

LEADING WARRIORS TO VICTORY

I am a warrior by nature. I do not shy away from confrontation or exhibit fear in the face of danger. I know it is boldness and authority the Lord put on me. In this ongoing spiritual battle with the enemy, God positions us so that we always emerge the victor. We only need to know our identity in Christ and stay ready with our Spirit-power tools.

Tools of Engagement

God has equipped us with warrior weapons to employ against the enemy. Their purpose is to ravage his camp and set people free from their bondages and oppressive conditions so they can worship and serve God in liberty. We would like to share some of these Spirit-empowered tools.

Rest

One of the most important tools I have learned to utilize is the simplest of all weapons, and that is rest. Yes, we can actually learn to rest when we encounter fierce engagement and apply it in our everyday struggles. As Graham Cooke, British-born prophetic speaker and author, often says, "Rest is a weapon."[40] I love that. For a warrior, this is actually a life-transforming truth. From Graham I learned that the enemy does not know what to do with a confident foe at rest. Satan's radar is set for agitation, and he is especially drawn to fear. Hell's hordes will always seek to tempt us to respond in angry agitation and fear to life situations.

Learning to rest in God's love, however, will assure us a place of repose as He turns it all around in our favor. Responding in rest to outbursts of anger, chaos, or confusion actually gives us the advantage as we receive Heaven's wisdom for the next move to make. Rest has a way of bringing calm, even to the most unsettling situation.

Compassion that Heals

Illness and torment are the weapons of the kingdom of darkness. Praying for the sick, and those tormented by satan, takes the weapons right out of his hands and uses them against him. Compassion goes after those afflicted in body and soul and overturns warehouses of ammunition stored for use against people under enemy attack. Employing these weapons turns curses into blessings, exchanges beauty for ashes, joy for mourning, and praises to God in place of heaviness.

---

[40] Cooke, Graham. *Qualities of a Spiritual Warrior,* Brilliant BookHouse LLC, 2008. Book 1 of 3 in a series: *The Way of the Warrior,* Chapter "Rest: The Warrior's Greatest Weapon," (pg. 38). brilliantbookhouse.com.

Because we carry Jesus' life in us, we release life and displace the works of the enemy who only brings sickness and disease, death, and the curse of destruction. Everything satan touches dies or begins to die; whereas, we release the life of Jesus to every person with whom we engage, thereby reversing the curse of satan's works of sickness, dying and death. And, best of all, we do it effortlessly.

It is Jesus' compassion ignited within us that initiates His healing power through us. All we have to do is radiate the brilliance of His Kingdom by intentionally switching on His light in darkness wherever we go and into whatever we do. Someone we will meet today needs prayer, and they will encounter Jesus' compassion through us. We only need to maintain an expectancy and stay alert in order to cooperate with the Holy Spirit who is setting up our next divine appointment to release compassion that heals.

The Blood, our Testimony, Surrendered Lives

Revelation chapter twelve describes three powerful weapons that ensure victory to warriors no matter the situation:

> *They conquered him* [the accuser, satan] *by the blood of the Lamb, and by the word of their testimony, and they did not love their lives in the face of death.* (Revelation 12:11, HCSB)

When a warrior is equipped with these three, people and nations will be released from darkness into light. The blood of Jesus will cause the enemy to flee, our testimony establishes the goodness of God as a witness against unbelief, and a surrendered life is the uncontested proof of love going the full distance no matter the cost. The enemy has no weapon against such tools.

Revelatory Word

The Holy Spirit further equips us with supernatural revelations through His gifts with a word of knowledge or word of wisdom that can literally disarm the enemy who has set up defenses in a person's heart. Utilizing these tools will allow the Spirit of God to penetrate a hardened heart with His love so it can receive salvation. The following is a testimony of a time the Holy Spirit exercised me in hearing Him and speaking what I heard.

A Word for a Fireman

I was out walking and praying one day in my neighborhood. I often would ask God about what He was doing in each house and how I could partner with Him. God had been training me to hear Him more clearly and He would often give me a specific word of encouragement for family, friends, and neighbors. On this day, I heard Him ask me to tell my next door neighbor these words, "I miss you, especially when you used to sing to me." To me this was cryptic and, quite honestly, a bit embarrassing as I imagined myself saying this to him. My neighbor was a big, husky fireman with four boys. I would often hear him bellowing out orders to his kids like a drill sergeant, and this word of knowledge didn't seem to fit his profile. Nevertheless, I rehearsed God's message, and I also rehearsed my neighbor's potential responses back to me. Because of my fear, I postponed giving him this word for several weeks.

Just a few days before I headed on a mission trip to Mexico, God was insistent that I deliver His message to my neighbor immediately. I was hedging but told God, "All right. If Aaron is in his backyard when I go outside, I'll call him to the fence." This took some real courage on my part. Swallowing my pride, I headed outside to wait and see what would happen.

Pretty soon, Aaron came outside and was working close to my fence trimming his shrubs. I moved over to where he was and started up a conversation.

"Hey Aaron!" I called, catching his full attention. "How's it going?" I rested my arms on top of the fence we shared, my insides churning. Small talk ensued.

"Aaron, I am a Christian . . . one of those Christians God speaks to . . . you know, like a friend would talk to another friend." I swallowed, looking to see if he was following me. I couldn't tell, so I just continued.

"So . . . uh . . . well . . . I, uh, I was talking to God awhile back, and . . . uh, He gave me a message to deliver to you . . ." I waited to see his reaction. He was just staring at me, so I pressed on.

"He said to tell you, 'I miss you . . . especially when you used to sing to Me.'" As I delivered the message, Aaron was still staring back at me, only now with a stunned look of shock. His face got red, his mouth gaping open, then he broke our gaze and returned to trimming his shrubs.

Turning back a moment later, he yelled over the fence, "Well, what am I supposed to do with that?" I really did not know what to say to him in response and just figured God would sort it out. I was relieved that I had finally obeyed the Holy Spirit's leading and delivered the message.

While in Mexico on my mission trip, the Lord spoke to me again about Aaron and said, "He used to be an altar boy in the Catholic Church and sang so well they used him for many of their events." No more information from the Holy Spirit was given, but then I understood the message God had given me weeks ago.

Upon my return home, it was Aaron who called me to the fence and asked, "What did you tell me that day when we spoke? I had just consumed two beers and was not really able to get what you were saying."

I repeated the message again, but this time added, "God told me that you were an altar boy and sang for many events."

The shocked look on his face said it all, "That is true!" We talked about his religious upbringing and life experiences.

"Aaron," I asked, "in all the religious practice as a Catholic, did you ever acknowledge Christ's crucifixion for you personally?"

"No," he answered, "it was all tradition."

"Would you like to do that right now?" With tears in his eyes, Aaron followed me as I led him in a simple prayer standing together at our backyard fence. He turned his life over to the One he used to sing about. Shortly after this, he began taking his wife and sons to a neighborhood community church.

This experience really taught me so many valuable lessons about hearing God and spiritual warfare. In partnership with Heaven's weapons of love, we take territory from the enemy camp in a framework of adventure and delightful fellowship.

Praise, Worship, and Declarations

We often employ the power tool of praise, worship and prophetic declarations as one of the most effective means to blast through walls of resistance. The bond of intimacy between the Lover and the Beloved will render the enemy powerless and cause him to flee away in terror. Exercising thanksgiving to God through praise and worship in the midst of a crisis establishes an atmosphere of faith and exclusive trust in the Lord who is our Victor. His favor on us has determined we are already victorious! Declarations of God's truth, therefore, have the power to overturn any atmosphere contrary to the mind of Christ and His kingdom.

There are situations that demand extreme worship. What does extreme worship look like? It will be different for each of us. I (Ron) will engage in a highly physical worship activity—praise music blaring—as I dance before the Lord or use my "war" flags, until I sense a release in my spirit. For me, this always breaks through confusion and fuzziness of mind and emotions.

In recent years, we have seen more and more 24/7 prayer and worship centers open up in churches and communities around the world. It reflects the passion of God's people to connect with the strength of His presence. The power released from centers of this type is making a huge impact.

Our focused and intentional praise and worship initiates God's responses of healing, deliverance, and transformation. As we make prophetic declarations reflecting the Father's heart, to bless our families, churches, communities, and nations, the heavens are opened bringing answered prayer and breakthrough.

Establishing our hearts and homes as centers of prayer and praise is a powerful tool in our arsenal against the enemy.

Extinguish Fiery Darts

The only effective tool and primary ammunition the enemy can use against us is fear and anxiety. He will often simulate situations that stimulate a fear response in us and cause our hearts to faint so that we lose courage to war against him. These are fiery darts. What is a fiery dart? It can be an accusation, a lie, a mental image to create panic and fear, etc. Quench these fiery darts before they do damage by refusing all fear tactics. I call this "enemy interference."

How do we do this? When the enemy plays a fear scenario, stop the replay in your mind before it has time to create a fear response. Renounce it out loud, make a declaration of the truth to counter his lie, and declare your trust in God. In this way, we do not allow any fear to take up residence in our thoughts, and so we put out the fire of his dart. This will need to be a focused exercise in order for most people to change the habits of fear-based thoughts and the negative cycle they bring.

At times, it seems, we are more in tune with the lies of the enemy than the voice of God. The enemy may visually suggest a disaster scenario and play a "video" in our mind suggesting a tragedy in the family, a car accident, illness, a trauma that is about to strike, etc. These lying suggestions often come in living color with emotions to accompany them so that you can visualize it, smell it, and feel it. Then comes obsessive, fear-driven behavior as these videos play over and over in our minds, greatly affecting our emotions and actions. Fiery darts are intended to haunt and torment us into an anxious state of mind.

You will become adept at quenching enemy darts before they hit you. Then determine to expect the tidal wave of blessing from Heaven coming your way while the enemy camp screams in rage as you destroy his works with crazy faith. Boom!!!!! *Finito! They failed again!* The enemy's camp suffers loss of territory, shrinks in influence, and retreats while licking its wounds.

Remember, satan is on the run—not you!—and your appropriated spiritual gifts are growing into an arsenal of effective nuclear power in the Spirit as you are being exercised and maturing in intimate relationship with the Lord.

Power Punches

The greatest way to deal with the lies of the enemy is to counter with the truth of God's Word. You may want to memorize strategic verses so they become quick reflexes. In response to the enemies lies, we proclaim the following verses and corresponding declarations. We recommend you make your own proclamations, memorizing and utilizing key Scriptures that are especially meaningful to you for this season of your life. Adjust them as the situation demands.

1 John 4:18.

Perfect love casts out fear, because fear has torment.

I am in Your perfect love, and I am fearless.

2 Corinthians 10:4a.

Pulling down strongholds.

I pull down the stronghold of [name it].

2 Corinthians 10:4b.

Casting down demonic thoughts and evil imaginations.

I cast down all demonic thoughts [name them]

and evil imaginations [name them].

Colossians 3:3.

I am hid with Christ in God.

I am hidden in Christ and the enemy
doesn't know where I am.

James 4:7.

Submit yourselves, then, to God. Resist the devil, and he will flee from you.

I am submitted to God and I resist the enemy.

Ephesians 5:18.

Be [continually] *filled with the Spirit.*

I am filled to overflowing with Your Spirit.

Luke 10:19.

I have given you authority to trample on snakes and scorpions and over all the power of the enemy; nothing will ever harm you.

I have authority over **all** the power of the enemy.

Since Jesus has given us His authority over all the power of the enemy, satan has none to use against us. His primary tactic is terrorizing fear to paralyze us so we are not successful to destroy his works. Determine to walk fearless in your authority.

We have field tested commanding faith against enemy fear tactics launched against us. Satan will throw unexpected distractions to stimulate fear in order to stop us dead in our tracks. This happens most often as we have been engaged with people concerning their salvation during an outreach. It would be impossible to count the number of times we have had to quote Luke 10:19 to vicious guard dogs lunging to attack.

Noble Warriors

As I have studied the biblical characteristics of David and his band of warrior men, I find them favored of Heaven and branded by God to be poured out from a crucible of turmoil and distressing circumstances while representing His kingdom of peace and security. I determine to be that kind of noble warrior.

For me, there are no better examples of such warriors than the three mighty men in David's circle. How I long to be one of them! These noble warriors[41] became the 5-star generals who bore the solitude of exile with David during the eleven years he was forced to run from Saul. David did not experience relief from Saul's pursuit until Saul was killed in battle. Meanwhile, David's mighty men stayed with him through it all and continued with him after he was crowned king. The testimonies of their bravery in battles alongside of David continue to be a source of encouragement for us, warriors leading troops to victory against overwhelming odds.

The Champions of Israel

Role models for spiritual warfare are biblical champions, and I have taken my own inspiration from many of them. Those great men pulled from a power not their own, and we are doing likewise as we expand His kingdom on Earth. Here are a few of my favorites.

Joshua: God's General

Joshua is distinguished as the man who just could not get enough of the manifest presence of God.

---

[41] 2 Sam. 23.

> *The LORD spoke with Moses face to face, just as a man speaks with his friend. Then Moses would return to the camp, but his assistant, the young man Joshua son of Nun, would not leave the inside of the tent.* (Ex. 33:11)

It is very likely that God chose him to be the one to succeed Moses because he exhibited such passion for His presence. While it is true Joshua was an amazing warrior who rose to be the commander of the armies of Israel, when encountering God's presence, Joshua responded in humility by falling face down.

Caleb: "Man of Another Spirit"

The Scriptures refer to Caleb as "totally dedicated to the Lord" (Josh. 14:9), and "a man of another spirit" (Num. 12:24). Caleb did not look like everyone else in the crowd; He was different. God rewarded him with the strength of a young man in his old age. At 85, Caleb insisted on taking his mountain and was not content to let the younger generation fight the enemy for his inheritance.

> *I am still as strong today as I was the day Moses sent me out. My strength for battle and for daily tasks is now as it was then. Now give me this hill country the Lord promised me on this day.* (Joshua 14:11-12)

I have determined to live as a man with a "different" spirit.

David: Giant Killer

We know the amazing exploits of David, the shepherd boy. Long before he entered the battlefields of the soldiers to face off with the giant, David killed wild animals with his bare hands to protect his sheep. He had been exercised in courage. With a single stone, young David fearlessly brought down the giant on the battlefield, killing him instantly. He then took the giant's own weapon from him, beheaded him, and promptly dragged the head up the mountains to Jerusalem.

The question is, why did David drag Goliath's bloody head 25-miles up the mountains to Jerusalem? At the time, this was a Jebusite stronghold and would not actually become the Israeli capital until David was king decades later. The city of Gibea of Saul was Israel's capital at the time. However, David was soaked in the manifest presence of the Lord Almighty, and, functioning as a "seer," he undoubtedly was acting upon Abraham's prophetic act of paying tithe to Melchizedek, the King of Salem.[42] The city of destiny was being claimed by David as his inheritance, and the Jebusites were being given an eviction notice with the head of the Philistine champion as the earnest down payment of what would come. With this one prophetic act, David sent a message to the Jebusites, "I'll be back!"

Philip: The Revivalist

Philip traveled to Gaza to release an entire people from the kingdom of darkness through one Ethiopian eunuch. This eunuch happened to be the CFO of Queen Candace of the Ethiopian empire. He was a high ranking official in the courts of this influential African queen.

Philip was really busy doing an amazing work for the Kingdom in Samaria, holding revival meetings where thousands of Samaritans and Jews were getting healed, delivered, and coming to faith in the Messiah.

> *Philip went down to a city in Samaria and proclaimed the Messiah to them.*

---

[42]   Salem was the ancient name of the city of Jerusalem.

The crowds paid attention with one mind to what Philip said, as they heard and saw the signs he was performing. For unclean spirits, crying out with a loud voice, came out of many who were possessed, and many who were paralyzed and lame were healed. So there was great joy in that city. (Acts 8:4-8)

Then, after they had testified and spoken the message of the Lord, they traveled back to Jerusalem, evangelizing many villages of the Samaritans. (v. 25)

Then, right in the middle of those amazing meetings, the angel of the Lord directed him elsewhere.

An angel of the Lord spoke to Philip: "Get up and go south to the road that goes down from Jerusalem to Gaza." So he got up and went. There was an Ethiopian man, a eunuch and high official of Candace, queen of the Ethiopians, who was in charge of her entire treasury. (vs. 26-28)

Philip obeys and promptly leads this high ranking Ethiopian official to Jesus and baptizes him.

When they came up out of the water, the Spirit of the Lord, carried Philip away, and the eunuch did not see him any longer . . .

Suddenly, Philip experiences the wonder of "translocation" as God whisks him away to Azotus in the blink of an eye for more evangelistic outreaches.

Philip appeared in Azotus, and he was traveling and evangelizing all the towns until he came to Caesarea. (vs. 29, 40)

Philip was experiencing one of the greatest revivals in Israel's history in Samaria, and yet the Holy Spirit redirected him to go immediately somewhere else for the sake of one person. Why was this so important? God was concerned for the peoples of the vast kingdom of Ethiopia. So much so that He went after this Ethiopian officer who hungered to know the Truth. Philip found him sitting in a royal chariot reading Isaiah 53 in the Hebrew Scriptures, a prophetic description of the suffering Messiah. It is interesting to note that the eunuch understood how to read Hebrew and had secured a difficult-to-obtain scroll of the prophet Isaiah. God really set this one up! Then God sends Philip, direct from Samaria, running alongside of the eunuch's chariot so he could hear him reading the Hebrew passages about the Messiah. Philip asks the Ethiopian eunuch leading questions about what he is reading, and easily, like picking ripe fruit off of a tree, leads him to Jesus.

At the time the Holy Spirit led him away from his successful revival "ministry" to head for Gaza, Philip had no clue the mighty influence this single Ethiopian eunuch would have on the whole of Queen Candace's kingdom. Consider that through this one connection, the vast kingdom of Ethiopia, southern Egypt, the Nubian nation, and all of Sudan down into central Africa was converted to Christianity.

The lesson is: we are often unaware of why the Holy Spirit is directing us a particular way, perhaps with an unsettling urgency that seems as "crazy" as Philip's story. In His compassion, the Lord of the Harvest will go after one man to reach a nation, a region, or a continent, and He will send whoever is listening and has a willing heart to respond.

Warriors Take Risks!

Carol and I love how the Reverend Canon Andrew White, the Anglican Vicar of St. George's Church in Baghdad, Iraq, responds when someone gives him a fear-based warning, "Now, Vicar, you take care!" Living and ministering in war-torn Baghdad, his amusing response is always, "Take care? I take risks!"

Yes! That answers the many calls for the so-called "balanced" Christian life. In light of the heroic biblical accounts, I would have to redefine this term "balance." Instead of seeing balance, I find a crazy faith everywhere in the Book—risk-takers, and not "care"-takers. Men and women thrust into the fires of an advancing Kingdom of great magnitude, epic in scope. The jet stream of the Book, if believed, sweeps you into its current, sometimes head-over-heels. The results can actually be dangerous. They are always the material for good stories. Better yet, they are the tools of deliverance and freedom for reality-starved, bored people wandering about in the shadow lands of the "balanced" life on Earth.

I do not know of any successful warriors who did not take risks to win the battles they faced. I once heard a quote by Angus Buchan, a Zambian-born evangelist from South Africa, "If your vision doesn't scare you, it's not big enough!"

In this Kingdom battle, there's risk involved.

Warriors Radiate

Our mandate is to set people free from whatever it is that prevents their "mighty man" or "mighty woman," God-given identity to emerge fully. I believe we need to appreciate the greatness of the One we carry in us at all times as we intentionally radiate the light of God's kingdom everywhere we go. We are simply participating with the effects that will transpire around us as a result of just showing up in any situation. This is hardly warfare. Rather, it is the dispensation of the most powerful tools in our arsenal: crazy faith, compassionate love, and great joy. Wherever we go, we radiate Jesus, effecting the atmosphere.

When all is said and done, love is the spiritual nuclear weapon that sends the enemy camp screaming in defeat, leaving behind a landscape littered, not with victims of demonic warfare, but the ripe fruit of a Kingdom harvest.

What does "radiating the Kingdom" look like? Let me illustrate this with a testimony of what took place while Carol and I were doing something ordinary one day.

Healing in the Swimming Pool

My wife Carol and I went to our California community outdoor pool where she swam laps. We intentionally announced to each other as we entered the facility, "We carry and release Jesus' light in this place." I headed for the jacuzzi and noticed Angelo, an elderly gentleman I had met some weeks previous. He usually swam laps, but on this day, he was only flutter-kicking in his lane.

"Hey, Angelo!" I called out passing by his lane. "How are you today?" It was then that I noticed he was supporting one arm.

"Oh, not too good," he answered, "I can't swim laps today."

"Why not?" I answered, stopping to inquire about his condition.

"Well, last week, while working out in the gym, I tore my rotator cuff." Normally I would ask to pray for someone who was in obvious pain, but I felt from the Holy Spirit not to pray for him right at that moment.

"Oh, I'm sure sorry to hear about that Angelo," I said sympathetically and then headed for the hot tub.

Carol was prepping to enter the water as I lay back in the jacuzzi. I had a full view of the pool and could see Angelo trying to swim, but with only one arm. My heart went out to him, knowing he was in pain.

As Carol began to enter the water and moved into her lap lane, I heard that glorious Voice from Heaven whisper to me, "The water has now become a healing balm. As Carol begins to swim, I am going to heal Angelo." At that moment, I saw something wispy touch Angelo's shoulder, and was now on full alert with expectation.

Carol was on her second lap when, suddenly, I saw Angelo stand up, place his hand on his shoulder, and begin to rotate his arm in small circles. He had a look of great surprise on his face. Then he put his face into the water and began to swim, only now with both arms. It was halting at first, but with each stroke, the ability to lift his arm improved. He was soon swimming normally.

Now I was the one shocked! Standing straight up in the jacuzzi, mouth gaping open, I watched God heal Angelo as Carol swam her laps alongside of him. The pool had indeed become a healing balm and Angelo was completely healed! Side by side, Carol and Angelo swam.

Stunned, I got out of the jacuzzi and walked over to the end of the lap lane Angelo was now approaching.

"Angelo!" I called to him, "Angelo, I just saw God heal your shoulder!" He looked up at me trying to understand what I was saying to him, but it was clear he had with no frame of reference for this. I knelt down beside him on the pool coping.

"Angelo," I said again, "That is my wife over there swimming laps beside you and God has healed people through her. When she got into the water, I saw God touch and heal your shoulder! That's why you are able to swim normally!"

Still I could see that Angelo was trying to comprehend my words to him. "Oh, do you mean some kind of spirit or something?" he asked.

"No, I mean Jesus. . .Jesus healed you!" I explained.

"Oh, Jesus! He did?"

I bent down on both knees closer to him and shared several testimonies of healing we have seen over the last three years. Now I had his full attention. He reached his arm to me out of the water and said, "Please pray for me! I have a pacemaker in my chest and have an important appointment next week!" I took his extended hand and laid my other hand on his chest and prayed for complete healing in his body.

"Angelo, be expectant now!" I told him after praying. Carol was getting out of the pool now and stopped to greet Angelo who was still checking out his shoulder that Jesus had just healed.

These kinds of experiences are not an uncommon thing for those who expect to see God meet people's desperate needs.

Desiring all the Tools

When I see warriors fully equipped with God's gifts and sharing testimonies of their victories, I feel a rush of holy jealousy and know that someday, somewhere, I will need those very things. I desire all the available tools with everything within me. I know God also desires this, and it releases a holy jealousy to pursue the "more" that He has for me.

One of God's names is "Jealous," which aptly describes His nature to go after something He wholeheartedly desires to possess. When considering the tools of advancing God's kingdom, God has put a desire in me to jealously want them all.

A holy jealousy is very different from the evil sin of envy. The dictionary definition of envy is: "a painful, resentful awareness of an advantage enjoyed by another, joined with a desire to possess the same advantage." Envy is sister to covetousness, which according to the dictionary means, "to desire what belongs to another inordinately." Envy and covetousness may end up in crime as well as a sinful attitude, and theft is their fruit.

A holy jealousy, in contrast, is wholeheartedly going after the tools of the Kingdom that I am lacking and zealously desire. What does that look like? If I see someone possessing a greater passion of love for God or exercising gifts that are enlarging the Kingdom, I go after that anointing to be activated and exercised in my life as I partner with the Holy Spirit. The holy jealousy I speak of empowers a person, honors the one anointed, and serves His kingdom with an expectation of doing even greater things than ever before. I have a holy jealousy to be equipped with every tool from the Father's storehouse to further the Kingdom, and God will honor my zeal.

Ready to Activate

As fathers and mothers in the Church, we have the opportunity to train and mentor warriors of the next generation, to see them exercised in all the tools available, and encourage them to win all of their battles. The following are characteristics that mark a Kingdom warrior.

- Warriors bring breakthrough because God has anointed them to do so. They press through impossibilities to victory and deplete the enemy's storehouses.

- Warriors take back enemy territory to rescue the helpless and give hope to the hopeless.

- Warriors bring Kingdom reform and change so that people have an opportunity to encounter God outside of the box of their religious confines that will bring transformation, reverse curses, and bring blessing to their family, city, nation, and region of the world.

- Warriors displace the prevailing atmosphere of evil; they set up Kingdom rule in its place.

- Warriors radiate and transform deepest darkness into brilliant light.

- Warriors do not react to circumstances with fear-based responses but rather, they initiate faith-based strategies to overthrow enemy strongholds.

- Warriors stay ready to be activated and deployed. As an active duty soldier, he stays fully dressed and fully armed. This warrior is never caught without the weapon he needs to defend himself against attacks by carelessly engaging in civilian activities. He stays sharp, fit, alert, tuned in, and in a high state of readiness.

- Warriors stay detached from the world with its mind-numbing activities that would distract them from active duty. They do not allow their senses to be dulled because they have a passion to see and hear clearly all that their Commander will be giving to them. These will be briefed with strategies against the enemy and they maintain an expectation of full victory.

- Warriors stay on the offensive and never allow themselves to live in a defensive, victimized role. They also stay on the offensive for those God has given to them to protect from enemy attack.

- Warriors have trained themselves to hear God, to see Him move far on the horizon, and they stay ready to amass their troops to "go to war" at a moment's notice, leading them to sure victory.

Our role is to lead warriors to victory and they, in turn, are training others to do the same.

Whatever you do,
let it be the gripping passion
of your heart
where nothing and no one
will deter you from
its pursuit.

NO LIMITS

I n the Kingdom, there are no limits, because we love and serve a limitless God. He says, "Nothing is impossible for you!" We respond, "With You, there is nothing I cannot do!"

We are motivated by super-faith, not by fear. We are compelled by compassion, throwing lifelines of hope, and we are love-crazed because His joyful presence is always with us. God loves all peoples, and so we will go to every nation. There are no closed borders to us. Political revolutions and regional conflicts do not affect our mandate. Language, culture, race or religion will never be a barrier or an excuse to not go and demonstrate the Father's great desire for all to know Him.

Jesus said, "Go. . ." Lack of money to fund what is on the heart of God is not a valid disqualifier. Refusing all excuses, prejudices, and personal limitations, and with nothing but the "all clear!" green signal lights ahead, we run with His permission and full blessing to go to the nations and declare Good News. We do not need to fast 40 days or "wait on the Lord" to determine if this is a good idea or not. We are fully confident and continually assured of His love and presence in us to work through us as we love each and every person He brings to us.

Determining to throw off the self-restraints and live in the limitless potential of who God says we are empowers and fuels our resolve to hear the sound of His glorious praise in every tongue. Their new songs will be testimonies of how His love transforms hearts, heals bodies, restores weary souls, delivers the imprisoned, renews minds, rights wrongs and injustices, and prospers families with abundant blessings.

With no restraints or limits, we will change nations.

Counting the Cost

From early in my walk with Jesus, I (Carol) determined to follow Him no matter the cost or how impossible it seemed. I fell in love with Jesus, and nothing else compared. I determined to spend the rest of my life loving Him.

One of the first choices I had to make at the age of 18 concerned the direction of my life. I knew God was calling me to full time vocational missions to serve on a foreign field, but it was so contrary to what was previously expected of me. I had been pursuing music and art degrees at a California college and felt the Holy Spirit redirect me with an invitation into a greater career choice. Before the Lord, I carefully weighed these questions: *Will I be pressed by family pressures and temptations to live the "good life" with financial security? Could I trust Him to live a much simpler life somewhere outside of my birth nation where I will be utterly dependent upon Him to provide all my needs? Will I give God my talents and skills to further His kingdom in the nations of the world?* Against intense family pressures, I chose the latter.

What I "gave up" did not compare to what I received. I feel the pleasure of Jesus on me wherever I am and in whatever I do.

While some may feel we have wasted our lives, Ron and I can only say that it has been worth it all, and we would not trade it for any other life. Misty Edwards wrote a song which describes perfectly our life passion.

I Will Waste My Life[43]

I will waste my life, I'll be tested and tried.

With no regrets inside of me, just to find I'm at Your feet.

I leave my father's house and I leave my mother.

I leave all I have known and I'll have no other.

I am in love with You and there is no cost.

I am in love with You and there is no loss.

I am in love with You, I want to take Your name.

I am in love with you, I want to cling to You, Jesus.

Just let me cling to You, Jesus.

I say goodbye to my father, my mother,

I turn my back on every other lover and I press on,

Yes, I press on.

In this love relationship with Jesus, there is no cost. The testimony of our lives as we have walked with Jesus forty-three years is that He is always good, He is always faithful, and He is more than enough for all we need.

Responding to the Holy Spirit

I remember the day when the Lord woke me up and said, "I want you and Ron to walk through Europe and pray." *That's it?* I

---

[43] "I Will Waste My Life" words and lyrics by Misty Edwards. Copyright 2010, Forerunner Music. MistyEdwards.com.

thought, *just pray?* That seemed pretty crazy . . . to just pick up and travel around Europe without much pre-planning, but then, God-ideas began to unfold. We sensed we were to go there for a focused 40-days, to pray through every nation, and stay loose so the Holy Spirit could lead us day by day. I initiated the first steps, God confirmed those actions, and with it came a forward momentum and confidence of His leading for the upcoming God-adventure.

I have learned that being responsive to the Holy Spirit is the one thing He requires with His leading. As we do, our senses will be sharpened with heightened clarity and expectation to see and hear directions for the next step. For this reason the Holy Spirit will put us through life lessons to exercise our senses.

In the book of Revelation, Jesus expressed deep concern that His church had become deaf and blind to His overtures. Seven times Jesus said, "Anyone who has an ear should listen to what the Spirit says. . ."[44] What we do for Jesus is so much more than desiring to be obedient. We want to be marked as the generation who see Him, hear Him, and respond immediately because we passionately love Him.

Going the Distance

God trains us for whatever work He has assigned in the Kingdom. The Holy Spirit is such a wonderful teacher, and His instruction is often en route—not necessarily in a classroom, or even a safe environment. Through our years, Ron and I have had some memorable teaching moments, all of which were designed to push us beyond our own personal limits into God's limitless provision to complete the mission.

---

[44] Rev. 2:7, 11, 17, 29, 3:6, 13, 22, HCSB.

Exercising Faith

One of the exercises we participated in during our intensive missions training in the early 1970s was a 3-day "faith trek." In this exercise, we were to completely rely on God to provide our meals and housing, expecting His Spirit to lead us every day as we shared Jesus on the streets. The teams of two were assigned to a city they had never Been. Knowing no one and with no pre-arranged place to stay,[45] we were led by His Spirit. Exercised faith becomes a God-adventure testimony.

Three-Day Faith Trek

On my faith trek, I (Ron), teamed up with my Bible school training roommate and good friend, Stan. We loaded salvation literature in our car to use as we shared Jesus with people on the streets and door-to-door. One of the literature pieces was our missions newspaper with encouraging testimonies of field activities which we gave to those who showed interest.

Stan and I arrived at the city where we would be working the next three days and got right to work. We had been on the streets all morning and most of the afternoon sharing Jesus when a man came running towards us shouting and waving the ministry newspaper we had given him earlier. Breathless, he arrived at the corner where we stood and said, "Hey! Are you guys on one of those 'faith treks' or something?"

My friend Stan and I look at each other perplexed and replied, "Yes! But, how would you know that?"

"Well, I opened up the newspaper you gave me and saw this article," he said as he held it up for us to see.

---

[45] The women of each team had pre-arranged homes to stay in but they were dependent upon God to provide their meals.

Stan threw his head back and let out his inimitable belly laugh. We honestly did not know that inside the newspapers we handed out was an explanation of students learning to trust God for provision on a faith trek.

"You must come home with me," our friend offered. For the next three days, our host cared for all of our physical needs while we were occupied with Kingdom business leading many to Jesus.

Exercises to trust God supernaturally in our early years set the tone for how He would lead us the next four decades.

Eight-Day Trek in Cyprus

While living in Israel in 1982, we needed to leave the country to renew our visa. With two small children, we took a ship from the Port of Haifa to the island of Cyprus and experienced another unplanned "faith trek." Unfortunately, we failed to change our Israeli shekels into Cypriot pounds before boarding the ship and calculated that we barely had enough to pay for our food and housing during our 7-day stay on Cyprus. Yet God provided miraculously the whole time! As we returned by ship to Haifa on the eighth day, we had no money for the bus trip home to Jerusalem. On the ship, however, God had reserved another miraculous provision. A Christian we did not know spoke with us for some time, and as she was leaving said, "I feel God wants me to give you this for your family." With that, she pressed a crisp $20 bill into my hand. She had no clue about our needs.

Once we arrived at the Port of Haifa, we discovered that war had just broken out between Lebanon and Israel that very day and all the soldiers were being deployed by public transport. There were very few buses in operation, but we managed to get a bus to Tel Aviv. We could feel the fear and chaos all around us. Amazingly, we were the last four passengers to board the last crowded bus from Tel Aviv to Jerusalem. Arriving well after midnight, we discovered all the buses had stopped and all taxis were in service. There were throngs of people at the bus stops waving cars down trying to get home. Here we were with two small, hungry, and extremely tired children, little money, wondering how we would ever get home in such distressing circumstances. In light of the miraculous provision the previous eight days, however, we continued to trust God.

The best is always reserved for last it seems. Suddenly, a loud, rickety car drove up to our crowded bus stop, rolled down the passenger side window and a man leaned over announcing loudly, "Talpiot!!" That was our neighborhood, but strangely, no one else responded. I wondered later if it was because the car looked and sounded like it was about to fall apart.

"That's for us!" Ron said as he ran to the car. "Can you take us to Talpiot?" The driver just smiled, eyes closed, nodding his head up and down.

We were stunned that the throngs of people were not fighting for this ride as they had with all the previous cars that passed by. Ron got me and the children settled in the back seat as he jumped in the front. I began to wonder if the car would actually make it to our home, but in a flash, the driver took off, roaring full speed down the street. I laid my head back thankful to God for this miracle ride in the middle of the night on the eve of a war.

For the next 25 minutes, the jovial stranger with the wild, curly hair drove us through streets of Jerusalem we did not even know existed. We hardly recognized where we were the entire journey. We finally arrived home around 2:00 AM via a circuitous route of the Holy City. Our friendly driver refused any offers of money.

The strange thing about this story is that we never saw this man again in our small neighborhood even though he told us he lived there. We looked, and listened, for that noisy car for weeks afterward. We finally realized that God had provided an angel to get us home on the eve of the Israel-Lebanon war.

We have come to appreciate that those who trust God exclusively will experience miraculous provision.

Cloud By Day, Fire by Night

After our unplanned and hasty exit from Israel in 2007, leaving behind family and ministry to return to the USA, we were homeless. This, too, provided many new adventures of Father personally caring for us. During this season, we determined to completely depend upon the Lord to lead and guide us every single day. It became a fun adventure as we sensed the cloud of His presence moving, or staying. Though this was one of the most difficult periods of our lives, it was comforting to see God's goodness follow us every moment. We realize now that this too was part of our training exercises for what was yet ahead.

Three-Month Europe Train Trek

In 1980, Ron and I traveled with a team of ministers and missionaries through Europe and the UK for 3-months by Eurail, the European rail system. On this trip, we traveled with our 3-year old daughter, two small bags, two backpacks, and my guitar. That was it. We were en route to live in Israel where we would minister the next four years and decided to join the team to see first hand what God was doing on the continent. This trip gave us invaluable lessons, and we learned so much about team dynamics, street ministry, living super-simple, God's provision, and exercises in the leading of the Holy Spirit.

Every day on that trip through Europe, God brought Ron

and me Jewish people and Israelis to meet, just to confirm, "this is the way . . . walk in it!" It was a vivid lesson of God's leading even when we were not sure if we were making the right choice or were in the right place at the right time. We have learned that He always gives signals along the path that are clear indicators to confirm, "You're on track! Keep going!"

Europe: 40-Days-to-Pray

Here we go again! Exactly 30 years later, and God asked us to do another impossible mission. When we first received the word to go to Europe and pray for 40 days in 2010, we did not have the money in our bank beyond our present month's bills. We knew this mission would have to be a supernatural provision, and actually, that got us excited. It was exciting to watch it all unfold.

Meanwhile, confident in God's leading, Ron and I pressed forward and began to plan the trip. One day while praying, the Lord showed us the connection: He had led us through Europe exactly 30 years before, and He wanted us to get a sense of the present spiritual climate so we can pray for these nations more effectively. There is value in being on the ground to see and hear firsthand what God is saying about the region.

In prayer preparation, we purchased maps of Europe, studied the Eurail route, made connections, and dream-planned the itinerary, keeping it loose. It would be nearly 50-days that we would be in Europe altogether. We started in Finland, 120 miles south of the Arctic Circle, went as far west as Swansea, Wales, prayed across the UK, flew to Paris, and trained to southernmost Spain. From there we took the ferry across the Mediterranean Sea to Morocco and returned back into Spain. An important part of our prophetic prayer journey was to travel through Andalucía where Islamists had once conquered Christian Spain, even changing its name. From Spain, we wove our way across the continent of Europe by train, ending up in Turkey during the middle of Ramadan. We literally hit the four corners of Europe and beyond.

Through the planning, we kept to our core values of "We serve a limitless God!" and "There are no limits, no borders." An attitude of "Everything is possible with God!" makes for easy planning. When we were stumped with "How do we...?" God responded with His peace, "I'll show you." Living life in relationship with a God who is compelled by compassion is a daily love adventure! Our mission would be marked by His heart of love for all people.

On this journey our mandate was to bless and pray for people everywhere we went, intercede in the 24/7 prayer rooms across Europe, pray in the oldest churches, sing in synagogues and the Jewish communities, make declarations around the oldest Mosques and Arabic-speaking communities of Europe and the UK. We spent a week in Oswiecim, Poland (adjacent to Auschwitz-Birkenau concentration camp) participating in an annual conference there. This was particularly important to us since we have worked with Jewish people for 40 years.

This trip was one of the most thrilling adventures we have ever done. Every day we experienced Holy Spirit connections while He took care of the details: where we would go, what we would eat, and where we would sleep. Through this trip, we sensed we were being trained for something much greater in our future. So many exciting testimonies[46] from this mission simply proved that God loves to walk with us through every ordinary and seemingly impossible situation. It is just fun to partner with Him as He works everything out for our good, and always in our favor.

---

[46] We kept a journal of our Europe mission with testimonies and photos. Visit the blog site: europe40days2pray.wordpress.com

Limitless Resources

There has never been a time when God led Ron and I to do something significant for His Kingdom where we had everything we needed up front to fully accomplish it. Rather, it required that we partner with God every step of the way to see Him provide supernaturally. The exciting part of the journey is to watch the Lord lead us, confirming His direction and assignment again and again, provide through unexpected means, and prepare the way ahead of us.

And yet, even en route to a mission, we encounter a number of difficulties that could be deterrents to discourage or cause us to doubt, fear, or wonder if we had made the right decision. Important keys to know in these times is that God loves us, is for us, and the Holy Spirit is leading us even when we do not know we are being led. Learn to rest when things are out of our direct control or when everything seems to be going wrong, knowing God is about to turn it all around with His goodness and provision.

Our surrendered life allows for a Holy Spirit-initiated exercise proving again and again God's limitless generosity as our sole provider. We have learned there is no end—or budget—to His resource availability. Once we throw off the self-imposed limitations of doubt and fear, retrain our mind to trust God, and appropriate His generous provision with crazy faith, we have all we need for exploits that advance His kingdom.

Finish, and Finish Well

A race doesn't count unless you finish. And in the Kingdom, it only counts if you finish well.

> *Well done you good and faithful servant.* (Matthew 25:21)

For several years I (Carol) worked as the Executive Personal Assistant to Derek Prince in Jerusalem and London. It was a great privilege to work with such a father in the faith the final years of his life. Derek often made a statement that really impacted me: "Many have a good beginning, but few have a good end." Through the years, Derek's words have come back to me again and again, and his words have helped to reorder my priorities as I evaluate my work before the Lord. I determined when I first heard Derek say this that I would have a good end. . .I would finish, and I would finish well.

Some believe that as we get older we should slow down, take it easy, rest on our laurels, and appreciate our accomplishments. In other words, sit back and watch the world go by as we listen to the young warriors tell their stories. But, Ron and I are not content to live life passively, and we have no plans for retirement. More and more we are coming to understand that God often reserves the best for last. Knowing this, it is vital that we maintain a heart attitude and a will to run to the very end, and not call it quits when we should still be going strong in Kingdom business. We have determined not to just endure to the end, but to run to the finish line. To do this, we must keep ourselves prepared and fit—body, soul, and spirit—so that we finish our course in full, matured faith. Crazy faith will actually intensify the training so that you can run faster, stronger, and with more endurance than ever before. We want to lead by example for the next generation.

We have really come to appreciate the value of keeping our physical bodies in good health and in shape so that we are not suffering with diseases and aging ailments that slow us down. It is our bodies, after all, that house the Holy Spirit, and must keep us going strong until God takes us home. Those who frequently travel overseas on short-term mission trips and those who are vocational ministers and missionaries must be in tip-top shape as they often endure severe conditions in foreign lands.

Enduring to the end is more than putting up with life's

difficulties. It has more to do with maintaining the whole person—a fit body, a healthy soul, and a vibrant spirit—to endure whatever comes our way. How well I know what it is like to live in war conditions (spiritual hot zones as well) and the stresses and demands it puts on the body, mind, emotions and spiritual life. It is tempting to give up under such circumstances. The Holy Spirit will always lead us into health, wholeness, and rest.

But I think there is another reason why we need to stay physically, mentally, and spiritually activated, even in our latter years. It is possible that the Lord reserves a special opportunity for Calebs who have kept themselves ready to take their mountain. Scouting out the Promised Land at a young age, Caleb did not see what the other scouts saw: impossibilities and giants. He only saw God's greatness. From that time onward, he determined that nothing was impossible for those who believed their God. Caleb lived his life without restrictions or self-limitations. We see Caleb again when the children of Israel were led into their land forty years later. He tells Joshua, "Hey, give me that mountain!" At this point, Caleb was 85 years old. Yet, he led a troop of young warriors up the high, rocky mountain terrain inhabited by giants. This was no small city, by the way. It was one of the most difficult cities the Israelites had to conquer.

That is the point. God will give such mountains inhabited by giants to those who have been conditioning themselves with super faith and endurance. The fact is, God gives more to those who have, not to those who have not. It may seem unfair, but that is the way it works in His Kingdom. He will partner with those who are ready to take the mountain He has reserved especially for them. God has provided limitless resources for all that is needed to ensure full victory and success. He saves the best for last for those who have trained themselves to live without limits.

Therefore, we strive to keep ourselves physically, spiritually, mentally, and emotionally fit for all God has yet ahead for us so that we finish, and finish well.

Live so in love
that nothing and no one
has the ability to offend you.

Love knows no sacrifice,
its reward is ecstatic joy,
our enduring possession.

In the end, love wins it all.

SIX

EXTRAVAGANT LOVE

When I (Carol) lived in Jerusalem, there was a woman who used to come to my neighborhood. She had no teeth, her hair was matted and dirty, and reeked of stale cigarettes. She had no underclothing and wore an old, worn tee shirt which you could see through. I was embarrassed for her.

She would accost every car at the intersection, banging on the windows, begging for small change. People avoided her, ignored her is more like it. I'm ashamed to admit that when I first saw her, I was repulsed, the same reaction as everyone else I suppose. I realized, however, that she probably lived in the adult center for the mentally disabled in my neighborhood.

That's when I decided to go after her and take every opportunity to just love on her. She was suspicious at first when I spoke to her kindly. It was almost like coaching a sparrow to sit on your finger. I felt her pain of constant rejection from people. With my interactions with her, my own heart begin to change. I was actually drawn to her. I loved her so much I would look for her every day. Slowly she began to trust me more and more. After a time, when she would see me far off, she would break out in a huge, toothless grin and run towards me for her hug. I always asked how she was doing, and we would have a nice chat. I was very concerned for her health because of her smoker's cough. I knew she was not well and wondered how long she would live.

After our visit, I would fill her hands with change I had reserved for her to buy a sandwich and a treat at our local mini-market, and off she would go grinning real big and waving goodbye. Her love for me, and gratitude for a small gesture of kindness warmed my heart.

I think God tests us by intentionally putting people in our lives that repulse us. He also gives us an opportunity to extend love and mercy to ones who are outside of our religious boundaries. These are ones we have determined, for whatever reason, are not worthy of God's kindness any longer because of their appearance, sinful lifestyle, or differing religious practices. We actually develop prejudices against people groups with a host of reasons that we justify. I have been guilty of all of these.

I am learning every day that God's goodness is so far reaching, much further than we are willing to go most of the time. The fact is, God Himself goes after the ones no one deems worthy to help, the ones who fall through the cracks: societal misfits, the helpless, the hopeless, the forgotten, those wearied and worn down, battered by endless waves of life's disappointments, betrayal, and loss. I feel the pleasure of Jesus on me when I go after these invisible people and love on them.

I volunteer to be one through whom God can express His far reaching, unconditional love, because He went after me.

Love Bears All Things

Our love is often tested to its extreme limits with an unexpected trauma. While living in Israel, we experienced the violent hatred of prejudice in a very personal way. A terrorist attack that succeeds is reason for celebration among Islamists. Even more, an attack against Jews in Jerusalem is the jewel in the crown of an Islamic terrorist group.

On June 11, 2003, I (Ron) became a companion in the suffering of the Jewish people in a single terrorist act.

After work, my mind was preoccupied, reviewing the events of the day as I waited at my bus stop with scores of Israelis returning home. It was rush hour.

Suddenly, an echoing blast ricocheted through the canyon created by the tall buildings in the heart of downtown Jerusalem. Before I could identify the source of the blast, or consciously know what it was, autonomic reflexes jerked my body into a half-crouched, self-protective stance.

As usual in a crisis, time slowed, and the next few seconds seemed to take place in slow motion. I looked up and realized that a suicide bomber had detonated himself aboard a bus standing one bus-length away from where I was waiting. The explosion had lifted the roof off the bus and it was just coming down again as I looked up. Then I heard what sounded like bullets whistling past my head coupled with large pieces of metal striking objects around me. I knew suicide bombers packed their bombs intentionally with screws, nuts, and bolts to maximize physical damage. Those projectiles are often soaked in arsenic which keeps the victim's blood from clotting.

The thought flashed through my mind, "You may die today!"

Loud crashes and sounds of metal pieces bouncing

123

off objects continued to whizz around me. Still frozen in place and unable to move, I opened my eyes and could see something pale and translucent between me and the bus. It seemed to be deflecting flying metal objects on both sides of my body. Something was shielding me.

I learned later that the Hamas terrorist had boarded bus number 14, disguised as an ultra-Orthodox Jew, and evidently, no one suspected him. Eighteen people died the moment he detonated his device.

"No one should ever have to experience this!" I screamed over and over again. Standing at the site and frozen in place, confusion took over. I could not think of what to do, or how to get home. *Should I sit down? . . . Should I walk? . . . Should I stop? . . . Should I wait? . . . Should I run? . . .* all crashed together in my brain. I could not make the simplest decision.

People were running in all directions to aid the injured, and I could hear people screaming and shouting. *Will there be a second bomb?* I wondered. Suicide bombers often work in tandem waiting until a crowd gathers to detonate a second explosive. I began walking aimlessly through the crowds of panicked people running every direction hoping to see someone I knew who could tell me what to do. My body felt as if chemicals had been dumped into my blood stream. Anger, helplessness, rage, and confusion all took turns cycling rapidly through my system.

I began walking . . . walking . . . walking . . . but I did not know where I was going. Finally, after half an hour or so, I reached my wife by cell phone; incoherent, I could not tell her where I was in the city.

"Ron, can you walk to the train station?" I heard Carol talking, but my mind was in shock and not functioning.

"Ron, can you hear me? Walk to the train station...do

you think you can do that?" she asked. "One of the guys will pick you up there."

It was a relief to see two of my children's friends at the train station, and they helped me into the car. When I finally arrived home, someone noticed I had pieces of human flesh pasted to the back of my shirt. How it got there, I still do not know. I never felt anything, yet it struck me hard enough to remain glued to my shirt all the way home. Once again, I appreciated God's protection. I could just as well have been struck with shrapnel from the explosive device, or pieces of metal from the bus.

At the sight of human flesh on my shirt, my shock broke into hysteria. A deep grief settled over me as I tried to reconcile how anyone could perpetrate such an act against other human beings. I could not stop the wracking sobs. My family called a doctor, and I was sedated. That day, the process of dealing with "Post Traumatic Stress Disorder" (PTSD) began, something the Israeli medical system have, unfortunately, become experts in treating.

As I considered my miraculous protection and survival of such a horrendous act, grieving for the 18 Israelis who died that day was a natural response and a way to deal with such agony of my soul. I sat shiva[47] along with these families for a full seven days. It helped me to mourn with them as I worked through the shock of trauma.

Experiencing terrorism in such a personal way only confirmed my resolve and commitment to the Jewish people. Living in the midst of Israelis for 20 years has allowed us to weep with His people in their times of pain

---

[47] "Shiva" is a 7-day Jewish mourning tradition where the mirrors of the house are covered, the men do not shave, and mourners sit on the floor instead of comfortably on couches.

coupled with God-ordained opportunities to direct their hearts to the only One who comforts.

The next week I walked into a mini-market in the center of town, one that I frequented from time to time. I put my drink and snack up on the counter with the exact payment. The shopkeeper stared at me for an a long while and said, "Ron, you're part of the club now."

"The club?" I asked. He was taking my shekels and ringing up my order. Handing me the receipt, he stared deep into my eyes.

"Four years ago," he began, his voice growing quiet, "I was standing at a bus stop holding my little boy's hand when a terrorist detonated himself. I watched my son disintegrate before my eyes." Tears filled his eyes and he turned away. I was immediately transported only one week previous to the bus bombing scene once again.

"After the bus exploded last week," Itzhak continued, "you came into my shop." I was in shock that day, so I did not remember doing this.

"Now you are part of the club," he repeated. There was an instant bond between us and my heart went out to him for his terrible loss. Transported into another PTSD daze, I found it difficult to walk home. Later that week I visited one of my neighbors. She expressed concern for my recovery and asked how I was doing.

"I'm okay," I answered, "some days better than others."

"Are you leaving us?" she asked, tears filling her eyes.

"Leaving? What do you mean, Shula?" I asked.

"Will you return back to America now and leave us— will you leave Israel?" she asked searching my face.

"Of course not!" I answered, dumbfounded that she

would ask such a thing. "This is my home, Shula! I love my Israeli friends . . . and Israel!"

With that she patted my arm in relief and said, "Good. We were all afraid since the bus bombing that you and Carol would leave us."

Being baptized into the suffering of the Jewish people only burned a resolve in our hearts to love even greater. Carol and I viewed the movie *Shindler's List* when it first came out in a Jerusalem theater filled with Israeli Jews. Many of them had been affected by the Holocaust in a deeply personal way. After the film was over, no one moved, and all of us were weeping. Carol and I looked at each other in that moment, and with unspoken words communicated, "This is why we are here."

Blinded by Extravagant Love

For years after the bus bombing, I suffered with PTSD episodes. I had to see a psychologist for about six months afterwards. I cannot count the times that certain sounds or smells would transport me back to that fateful day.

Six years later, anger against the murderer still seethed deep inside me. I had successfully suppressed it and would deny it if anyone would have asked me directly. But I knew it was a time-bomb deep in my soul.

After my awakening Throne room experience in 2009, I loved my long daily walks with Jesus and would just get lost in adoring Him. During these times I would sing and worship out loud for hours along hiking trails near my home.

Some months after the vision, I had been on one of my walks in a deep place of adoration for a few hours. Suddenly, in that deep place, the Lord brought the face of the homicide bomber right in front of me like a holographic image. It was so real I felt as if I could reach out and touch him. I could feel the eyes of the

Lord looking into me and asking, "What is going on inside?"

I was stunned. In that moment I realized there was no more hate! Nothing was agitating me as it usually did when the subject would come up. Pure and holy God-given love flooded my being. I forgave the bomber in that moment and told God that if he were standing right there in front me, I could actually hug him and really mean it. I knew the bomber was as much a victim as I had been. The fact is, young men, recruited by a handful of hate-filled terrorists, are told they will bring their families riches and honor by giving their lives in such manner.

That day, heaviness left me that I didn't even know was there. Freedom and liberty took up residence in my spirit.

Arrested as a Terrorist

Many varied experiences shape who we are and often bring a paradigm shift in character. At the onset, it may appear to be a terrible experience, but love for the people and nations God calls us to chooses to see His goodness in any situation as we take up our post on their behalf. The following is such an example.

My (Ron) airplane flight from Israel to Belgium landed in Brussels. From there, I took a train to London where my missionary friends met me. The war between Israel and Lebanon in the summer of 1982 was still raging, and I had been sent on this mission by a team of my colleagues in Jerusalem because of growing, worldwide anti-Israel media bias. The Israeli Ministry of Foreign Affairs provided fact-based videos, and instructed me to go to the World International Zionist Organization in London to convert the videos for use in America.

We made our way across London to Golder's Green, the London Jewish community, but had difficulty finding the address. My missionary friend drove around and around in circles trying to find it. Finally, I got out and knocked on the large front door of a Jewish school to get some information. Strangely, they refused to open the door more than a crack. I thought it was an odd response.

We finally did find the correct address, took care of the video exchange, and headed back across London.

Suddenly, out of nowhere, our van was cut off and surrounded by unmarked London police vehicles. Armed police swarmed our car shouting at us, "Get out! Get out of the car . . . get out now!" My two friends quickly exited from their front doors. I felt hands drag me with great force over the front seat and out onto the pavement. Picking me up, they roughly shoved me against the side of the van.

With my face pressed against the van, I called out, "Hey, what's happening?" I was trying to make logical sense of it all. "What's going on?"

"Shut up! Just shut up!" came the answer as police handcuffed me and gruffly shuttled the three of us into separate police vehicles.

Down at Golder's Green London precinct, my friends and I were processed and promptly put into three separate jail cells. My mind was whirling as I considered why in the world we would be arrested and put in a London jail. I could hear my friends in the adjoining cells as the hours went by, when suddenly, one of them began to sing a Spanish chorus. My missionary friend to Guatemala picked up in strength and boldness as his clear tenor voice rang out praises to God. But quite honestly, I could not see the correlation of us in this London jail cell and Paul and Silas.

Finally a policeman came and asked, "Who's the leader of this group?"

"That would be me, I suppose," I offered. They promptly took me to the Sargent on duty and the questioning began.

"Why were you running from the police?" he demanded.

"What? I was not running from the police. Why, I had no clue that a compact white car would be a police vehicle," offering my honest explanation. The police vehicles in Israel were very different.

The Sargent pointed directly at me and said very sternly, "Sir, did you know that you came within a few seconds of us shooting you in the back of the head?" Now they had my full attention.

"What is this all about, officer?" I asked. To my left, I could see several policemen rummaging through my personal effects all spread out on the table. In my briefcase I had the videos given to me by the Israeli Foreign Affairs office to use on my 3-month trip to the UK and America. I realized in that moment how incriminating the titles were: "The PLO in Lebanon," "IRA Training Camps under Yasser Arafat," etc. The police officer was now holding up my airplane and train tickets as proof I was indeed the terrorist they had been looking for. It seems that I had landed in Brussels, Belgium, the very same day a synagogue there had been bombed.

Come to find out, the London Jewish community where we had driven through that morning had been on high alert for a week since a terror attempt had been made against the school where we had stopped. Unbeknownst to us, it was the elementary school for the children of Israeli diplomats. For their protection, police had installed a closed-circuit TV camera in their parking lot and they had watched us arrive and me get out with my briefcase. Now it all seemed to make sense why the school only opened the front door a crack. Apparently, the terrorist had also landed in Brussels on the very same day that I did, and had taken a train to London also the very same day . . . mistaken identity.

The irony of it all . . . here I was in London attempting to show the world the real situation of Israel's need to defend themselves against terrorism, and I was the one arrested as a terrorist. They extended their apologies to me as they realized they had the wrong man.

"Before I go," I said to them, repacking my briefcase, "I would like to thank each one here for the careful protection of the London Jewish community." Having just come from Beirut, Lebanon, seeing firsthand the results of the war there, and living in Israel with terror attacks, it was a relief to know the London police were protecting the Jewish community. I blessed them in their efforts.

The Lord Gives, the Lord Takes . . .

Sometimes, in our God-mission, we can be terribly misunderstood by the very people we are called to love. Occasionally we are accused of wrongful actions and considered their enemies. Situations arise where we must simply trust the sovereignty of God and His extreme, radical love for us.

One of the most difficult things we have to do in life is to release the very thing God has given to us. After 16 years of serving in various capacities, we were asked by the Israeli Ministry of Interior to leave the country. Under a false accusation of "illegal" missionary activity, we were given 12-days to exit, requiring that we leave behind nearly everything we owned. To our shock, a story with our photographs made the front page of the Israeli newspaper "The Jerusalem Post" Friday edition with the headline: "Evangelical Pastor Kicked Out of Israel." This created quite a stir at the online site of the Post with hundreds of comments, as well as over 60 international websites that carried the story. Where we had hoped to slip out of the country quietly, this was not the case. Many of our Israeli friends came to our defense and were incredibly supportive.

As we were being strip-searched at the Tel Aviv airport in the police holding area, the items from our suitcases stretched out on long examining tables, we turned to the 15-man team of Israeli security personnel and blessed them. We determined that even in this misunderstanding, our friendship to their nation would be ongoing. Many of them were in tears as we were escorted out of Israel under armed guard.

Yes, our love can be misunderstood. A couple of years later, as Ron attempted to return to Israel for a short visit, he was promptly jailed and again escorted out of the country under armed guard.

Sometimes God asks us to give up everything with no answers why. It may be that we will never fully know why we had to walk such a difficult path during a particular season of life. Yet, there are other times when God allows us to understand the reasons much later. We realized within a few short years, had we not left Israel in such a way, we might not have been positioned for the next thing God had prepared for us: participating in the radical love outpouring in Islamic nations.

Learning to trust His sovereignty and love in the difficult moments, even though we do not understand why, is the best posture we can take.

> The LORD gives, the LORD takes away. Blessed be
> the name of the LORD. (Job 1:20b)

Since that time, we have come to appreciate God's goodness to us, even in the most difficult times of His leading when we cannot see the reason or logic. The fact is, there is never a time when God is not good to us. Never! In the moment of our distress, confusion, and chaotic circumstances, His presence and love will quiet our hearts. Times such as these are an invitation to encounter God's embracing love though blinded by the "whys?" in our darkest night. We can trust His redeeming and restorative nature.

Releasing Forgiveness

We will have many times throughout our lives to release an offense that we have harbored. God will intentionally exercise us to extend mercy to those who don't "deserve" it; yes, even to an enemy. Releasing forgiveness has such power in our personal lives. For whatever reason we were offended, however justified it may be to harbor that offense, releasing forgiveness will free us and at the same time position us to receive God's forgiveness and mercy. In addition, it releases us from mental anguish and torment, reverses any destructive, residual effect upon our body and soul, and activates God's blessings into every area of our lives. Releasing forgiveness to the offender is that powerful.

Ridding our hearts of offense is the first step in softening a hardened, embittered heart that resulted from the subsequent circumstances of the offense and restoring us once again to a fervent, first-love relationship with Jesus. It is the only way we can walk in radical love, the kind of extravagant love of the Father that will bring transformation to families, cities, and nations.

God passionately loves you, me, and every single person He created. Jesus' shed blood proved that. Only those who have been forgiven can release forgiveness. Only those who have encountered His radical love can release radical love.

Therefore, we have determined to be radical, extravagant lovers of God and people—all people.

Even now,
heroes are walking the earth
and are already
positioned in every city.
These agents of transformation
are celebrating victory—
the Kingdom hot in their hands—
as they chase down breakthrough,
refusing to be denied.

CELEBRATE EVERY VICTORY

Every victory builds faith for the next impossible situation we will face. We can actually celebrate ahead of time as we recall the history of all God has done in our lives—His deliverance and provision through every overwhelming situation. For this very reason, God instructed the children of Israel to "remember". He knew that when they were faced with an army that outnumbered them, they would recall the day God destroyed Pharaoh's army and walked them through the Red Sea on dry land. For this reason the Israelites celebrate Passover every year, even to this day. We too celebrate the Lord's Supper in gratitude as we remember all Jesus did for us. Our confidence for victory is through the power of remembering.

Intentionally Thankful

Recalling God's faithfulness initiates thankfulness. An

intentional act of gratitude releases God's response in provision for all we need. Reviewing His goodness establishes a thankful heart and makes way for greater measures needed. Because of this, we can look at any crisis we face and declare with assurance and a heart of faith: "I remember what You did there. Therefore, I trust You for this today, God!"

In the face of the enemy's lies, thanksgiving is the truthful declaration: "God *is* good, He has *always* been good, He will *continue* to be good. God's goodness *will* follow me *all* the days of my life."

Thanksgiving is always the starting place of praise to God.

> *Give thanks to the Lord for he is good and His love endures forever.* (Psalm 107:1)

A declaration of God's goodness was the battle cry of the Israelites as the worshipers preceded the armed soldiers.

> *The Lord is good and His mercy endures forever...* (Psalm 100:5, NIV)

Thanksgiving is the purpose for every biblical pilgrimage feast where the worshipers brought tithes and offerings up to Jerusalem. Remembering God's generosity of provision stimulates joy. One of the greatest biblical festivals celebrates with seven days of joy.

The Season of Great Joy

As the harvest moon moved across the silent sky in Middle Eastern heat, I (Ron) couldn't help but think of the line in the Christmas Hymn, "Silent Night . . . all is calm, all is bright." Our annual family tradition was to lie under the palm branches of our "tabernacle" on hot Jerusalem nights during the 7-day

Sukkot festival and watch the full moon dance with the stars as it navigated its way across the sky. We would barely be able to sleep as the brilliance of the harvest moon filled our *sukkah* with golden-colored light, sending the shadows of the palm branches that covered the tops of the flimsy wooden structure skittering across our sleeping bags. Tradition has it that the roof of the *sukkah* must have branches loose enough to reveal the glories of God's heavens.

Hag Sukkot, Hebrew for "Feast of Tabernacles," is a fall festival of joy and rejoicing. The full moon was always the largest of the year—God planned it that way. Fullness. Joy. Sukkot is a memorial of the Israelites journey across the Sinai upon their hasty exit from the slavery of Egypt. Its celebration is an intentional act of remembering God's miraculous deliverance, His goodness, and His presence, with family and feasting in a celebrative atmosphere. This particular feast is often called the "season of our great joy" for good reason. It is an annual prophetic rehearsal of the final ingathering harvest at the end of the age. And on that glorious day, I imagine there will be thunderous responses over every single victory with joyous feasting and heavenly celebration.

We have always been intrigued by God's time piece of the biblical festivals.[48] I wrote a book called *The Feasts of the Lord*[49] where I explore much more about the deeper meaning of these prophetic celebrations marked by "remembering." As a new creation in Christ, we are presence-keepers, His laws written in our hearts. Memorializing God's intervention came well before the Law and was marked with a deep state of thanksgiving that included all the senses of the whole person: sight, smell, hearing, taste, and emotion. Memorializing God in this way goes

---

[48]   Lev. chapter 23.

[49]   Cantrell, Ron. *The Feasts of the Lord: The Feasts, Fasts, and Festivals of the Bible*, 2013, Revised edition. Available on Amazon. com.

several levels beyond thanksgiving. It builds solid memories that declare: this is what God did for me, to me, and through me.

Power Remembering

The Hebrew word for "memorializing" is *haga*. We will explore several meanings. The definition most appropriate to our subject would be, "meditate–power remembering." The opposite is forgetting, and the only allowable forgetting is where God forgives our sin and then forgets. Whereas, meditating (power remembering) upon the miraculous deliverance and provision God brought us can have explosive results. It is our personal testimony ramped up to turbo crashing into the dullness of Earth.

For instance, it was anything but a calm and silent night when the Angel of Death "rent the heavens" and exploded with deliverance. Every Egyptian household felt a painful loss as Moses moved 1.5 million people out of Goshen overnight. Even the wild dogs were stunned into shocked silence at this miracle.

> *But against the Israelites, whether man or beast, not even a dog will bark, so that you may know that God makes a distinction between Egypt and Israel.* (Exodus 11:7)

That which God does powerfully in our lives must never be forgotten but is to be erected as a memorial so that we, and generations after us, will remember. This one night of mighty deliverance became the testimony of God's people, and every nation around Egypt also remembered—a fearful reminder.

That's the power of remembering. As we meditate and consider the depth of God's intervention on our behalf— that benchmark moment in our life that transitioned us into transformation—it will have a potent effect on how we view our present crisis situation. Perhaps it is the testimony of when you first met Jesus, or when God came through miraculously for you in a hopeless situation. Recalling those circumstances and all God did to bring you through empowers you to declare in faith, "God, You will do that again for me. I trust You in this situation."

Testimony of the First Martyr

Stephen, standing before the Sanhedrin, retells the history of his people in great detail, including the story of the Exodus from Egypt.[50] What does the Exodus have to do with the crucifixion of Jesus and the subsequent outpouring of God's Spirit? Much! Even after the dramatic retelling of the history of the Jews, the life of Jesus, His death and resurrection, the crowds still stoned Stephen. However, in the backdrop, a man's spirit was being taken captive by the kingdom of God as Stephen memorialized Israel's history which included Jesus' life, death, and resurrection. Saul stood in the shadows aiding Stephen's murderers,[51] but shortly thereafter, had a life-transforming personal encounter with the Messiah. The life of Saul, now changed to "Paul," was launched by Stephen's "haga" moment that morning.

Stephen's testimony took Israel's glorious God-victories, memorialized and celebrated, linked them with the Messiah, and released a momentum into the Church that captured the hearts of both Jews and gentiles. Over the coming weeks, more than 8,000 Jewish people professed their faith in Messiah Yeshua in Jerusalem and were baptized! Consider this for a moment: a revival of that proportion would surely make headline news in any city of the world! Just this one incident alone refutes the accusation that the Jews rejected Jesus. Every strata of Jewish society was greatly affected.

---

[50] Acts 7.

[51] Acts 8:1.

This is the power of testimony and the effects are stunning. Nations surrounding Israel, with representatives in Jerusalem, also came to faith in the Messiah and were baptized. Severe persecution of the Church followed, immediately dispersing these new believers throughout the region with the Good News.

Another definition of *haga* is "to growl" or "roar like a lion." You can imagine that Stephen's sermon was not demure or subdued by any means. Because it was a major feast day, there were thousands of Jews and gentiles in the Temple area. A passage in Isaiah reminds us of what that moment might have been like. Stephen roared (*haga*) the message of the Gospel with great passion and zeal as the crowds of Jewish leaders and rabble-rousers responded, angrily shouting out their murderous threats. But the Lord of Hosts was right there with Stephen as he stood on Mount Zion.

> For thus hath the LORD spoken unto me, "Like as the lion and the young lion roaring [haga] on his prey, when a multitude of shepherds is called forth against him, he will not be afraid of their voice, nor abase himself for the noise of them: so shall the LORD of hosts come down to fight for Mount Zion, and for the hill thereof." (Isaiah 31:4, KJV)

As the angry crowds rushed him, Stephen raised his eyes to see Jesus stand up to receive him as he was being martyred.

Deceptive Age of Reason

Another meaning of the word *haga* is "to imagine." Our ability to memorialize God's goodness must utilize our imagination. Yet, from the industrial revolution of 1750-1850, this was stolen from the Church and replaced with the fear that using our minds through God's gift of imagination was "dangerous" and should be discouraged. At the same time, enthusiasm (i.e., enthusiastic about God) became a pathological illness. The word "enthusiasm" comes from the Greek "en Theos" or "God in you." In times past, people who became overly excited were thought to be crazy. The revolution ushered in what is known as the "age of reason," which taught if you could not see or feel it, it was not real.

A pamphlet was written and published about this concept called, "The Age of Reason: Being an Investigation of True and Fabulous Theology," by the American revolutionary Thomas Paine, and was a best-seller in the United States. The booklet challenged institutionalized religion as well as the legitimacy of the Bible. Paine advocated reason in the place of divine revelation (leading him to reject anything out of the realm of the "natural" such as miracles) and supported the view that the Bible was simply an ordinary piece of literature rather than divinely-inspired text. For the Church, who by this time had traded the power of her authority through the cross with adherence to religious disciplines out of fear of hell, Paine's booklet spelled freedom. The concept spread like wildfire and the deceptive age of reason began.

The print dates and popularity of this pamphlet was between 1795 and 1807. It is interesting to note that simultaneously, a polarization was happening in the United States and Britain, those who wanted to be free of religion versus a series of Great Awakenings. This period saw some of the largest revivals ever recorded beginning in the 1700s and continued on right up to the Jesus People Movement in the late 1960s.

There is a new wind blowing the atmosphere of Heaven into our midst and bringing with it the reconciliation of a redeemed imagination and enthusiasm. God's revelation along with miracles, signs, and wonders is displacing the "religion" of stoicism that crept into the Church under the guise of respectability. God is restoring the gift of our imagination so we are able to perceive imprints of His heart and creatively express them. The fact is, we all use our imagination a thousand ways through the day. Creative people, inventors, and others must "see" a thing before it can be actualized. But, as Christians, we have been reticent to accept anything from our imaginations, particularly as we commune with God. Let us consider that a renewed mind, rightly related to the Holy Spirit, can expect God will plant valuable and creative ideas for business and Kingdom advancement through our redeemed imaginations.

A Future Mindset

Another meaning of the word *haga* is "to devise," or "to plot." The dictionary definition of devise is "to form in the mind new combinations or applications of ideas or principles." Consider, for example, God's heavenly identity for you and the need to create a new mindset of His image in you. To do this, combine the past, present and future: God sees you in your future (perfect), combined with your past (forgiven), to erase all negative lies that continually assault your mind and affect your emotions (present). This new mindset has the potential to transform your thinking to celebrate your life as the victorious one He created!

Graham Cooke's transformational teaching[52] about this points out that God does not view us as we view ourselves. We often see ourselves in the present with all the past hanging on us like "Pilgrim's" backpack.[53] Rather, God sees us in the present with only our perfected future. We know He has already forgotten our past, so the enemy has no foothold there. Taking this to heart has a powerful ability to transform our thought processes into a new future mindset instead of dwelling on the failures of our past.

---

[52] Cooke, Graham. *Prophetic Wisdom*, (pg. 97). Brilliant BookHouse, 2010. Available online: brilliantbookhouse.com.

[53] From the classic book *Pilgrim's Progress*.

What's Passed is Past

Relating to God in this new reality of a future mindset can, at times, be quite humorous. I had to wade through it the hard way. It goes something like this:

Oh, God! Why am I like this? meaning, *Just look at the contents of the grimy backpack of my past.*

"Because I made you thus!" replies God, translated to mean, "You are the fire warrior I created for My kingdom on Earth!"

But, why did You make me like this? I answer back, thinking He is referring to the grimy backpack of my past.

"So you can take territory away from the enemy and set people free!" He explains excitedly.

What?! I respond incredulously. In Heaven's reality, God only relates to us from our perfect future because the grimy backpack of our past has been tossed forever into His sea of forgetfulness. He is not playing dumb by not remembering. Rather, He is gloriously liberating us from our past and drawing us forward into the perfect future of what He has prepared.

Heaven Celebrates Your Victory

God lives in Heaven's environment surrounded by continual joy and celebration. Explosions of praise shake the foundations of the heavenly temple over and over again. There is no negative introspection there, no contemplations of past failures. That would be, actually, the complete opposite of *haga*. The angels gather by the myriads in joyful celebration over our victories.

So, one day, you finally get it. The journey begins. You are equipped with Heaven's identity on you, but you still hear the lies of the enemy through reminders of your past. With what you know about your identity in Christ, however, you now are armed to the teeth. You jerk the enemy's little accusations into the perfect future, ram a fire sword of God's forgiveness deep into them, and then watch them melt in the fire hurricane of God's passion for you. You find new courage because you finally see yourself as the person God created you to be. You are already known in Heaven as victorious. Why, they have already begun to celebrate your victory! You can see them and hear them cheering you on. Joy explodes over you. *Boom!* Accusation vanishes.

The battle rages. The running and screaming begins, but it is not you running or screaming in fear. No, you are roaring (haga) like a lion! It's about time. You can feel the confusion of satan's camp as you advance, breaking through enemy lines to take back all he has stolen and deplete his storehouses. You almost explode with the atmosphere of Heaven and know the rest of your life will be different . . . so very different.

You've Already Won

You have a secret weapon against the enemy that is the confidence you walk in every day.

> *For you have died, and your life is hidden with Christ in God.* (Colossians 3:3)

When you are hidden in Christ, the enemy does not have a clue where you are or what you are going to do next. He is the one running scared. He is the whining one, not you. He now calls off the battle against you because every time he attacks, your counter-attack takes back territory—his territory. His attacks against you are counter-productive so he is leaving you alone now and going somewhere else where his devices work.

Heaven has birthed another warhorse who laughs at fear and charges ahead with trembling fury because he cannot stand still. At the trumpet blast, he snorts defiantly. He smells the battle from a distance; he hears the commander shout, "Advance!"[54]

Your need for strength will not be to fight the enemy but to host God's glorious presence. The absence of past skeletons, accusations, and daily battles with lies leaves a vacuum which now gets filled with God's strengthening Spirit, providing for unceasing communion. This is not petitioning, but rather, intimate fellowship with the One who calls us "friend."

God speaks in a thousand ways, and now you are clean and purified for tuned-in reception. He loves intrigue, suspense, surprises, valentines, spiritual candy . . . He is full of smiles and hugs and almost knocks you down backward with affection because He finally has your full-on attention. The Divine Three settle in for adventure: Father, Son, and Holy Spirit. You can hear them planning and scheming what will bring you joy and pleasure day by day. They sing over You. The Holy Spirit anoints your imagination with the oil of joy. You sometimes have to pull off the road and recover from the overwhelming presence and love celebrating over you.

It suddenly occurs to you that life no longer resembles what it used to be. Drudgery and boredom is just a memory. Each day is now stretching out before you filled with hopeful promise. We are heading up into the stratosphere with expectations of great adventures, and only God knows if there is any limit.

So, roar lion! Take your memories and memorialize (haga) His goodness to you and your family. Look out into the night sky and know there is no end to this eternal love. His purpose for creating you, the reason you are on Earth, is to discover it all in awe and wonder so that you will be filled with His pleasure.

---

[54] Rendered from Job 39:19-25.

Our life mandate is
to run after Him with
all that is within us
for the rest of our lives.
Nothing else
compares.

READY AND WILLING

As one out of the hippie movement reborn into the Jesus People, I (Carol) have lived my life as a "free spirit." I really love people, cultures, languages, and I'm always up for the adventure of exploring new things. I am flexible, adaptable, and can easily fit into the unexpected. It's a good thing because I never would have made it in the Middle East, where you come to expect the unexpected.

Christmas Mediterranean Cruise

I was cleaning up the dishes from our first Christmas dinner since we had returned to live in Jerusalem when the phone rang.

"Hey, did you have a nice Christmas?" Clarence asked. Clarence Wagner, Jr., international director of the Christian organization we were volunteering for in Jerusalem, led the team in social assistance programs and Jewish-Christian relations. I

147

was curious why he would be calling at such a late hour on Christmas night.

"Oh yes, it was really nice. How about you?" Ron and he chatted about their Christmas celebration. I could hear the excitement of our three children scurrying about the living room exploring their new gifts. As I finished hand washing the last of the dinner dishes, I picked up bits and pieces of the conversation between Ron and Clarence on the phone.

"Say, not sure if you guys are willing to do this, but I wondered if you and Carol could be ready to do a 10-day trip to Odessa, Ukraine, by ship . . . uh, tomorrow morning about 6:00 AM? A driver will pick you up, and we have arranged for someone to stay with your children," Clarence told Ron.

As it turned out, Ron and I had been selected to join a team of Christians for a very special and top secret journey aboard a Greek Mediterranean cruise ship. A Christian organization had hired this ship to make its way from the Port of Haifa in Israel, across the Mediterranean, up through the Turkish Bosphorus Straits and finally, to the Black Sea Port of Odessa. The trip would be five days there and five days back. The mission: bring back hundreds of Russian Jews who were waiting at the port to immigrate to Israel. On board the ship would also be a 15-man team of Israeli Special Forces, positioned because of the credible danger this voyage presented with its Russian Jewish passengers, along with a team of Israeli diplomatic officials who would be processing their immigration. We were to tell no one what we were doing or where we were going for security reasons. It was a clandestine secret journey with all the intrigue of a "mission impossible" movie script. There were three secret pilot journeys of this type, and Ron and I were selected to be on the second. The ship had to slip through the narrow Turkish straits, keeping its Israeli and Jewish "cargo" hidden for fear of reprisals.

"Yes, of course we'll do it!" Ron responded to Clarence on the phone. How could we not? Rescuing Russian Jewish people from the Communist regime, and returning them to their ancestral homeland has been our mandate the previous twenty years and it was one of our primary purposes in returning to live in Israel in 1991. We were already assisting the return of thousands of Jews from the former Soviet Union.

On board the ship to Odessa, we encountered the worst Mediterranean winter storms of the century. We all realized quickly that this would be anything but a leisurely pleasure cruise. Instead, we spent most of those five days cradling the toilet, overcome with seasickness. Even the IDF Special Forces team and the experienced Greek ship crew were seasick.

Nevertheless, the privilege of this voyage to help God's people return to their homeland, and the future potential of subsequent trips, was well worth every moment. We could write a book itself about this one mission. Every single family had a personal testimony of their miraculous journey from a remote village of the Ukraine, traveling to Odessa, and finally, to the Promised Land. We personally connected with many families on board and counted this as one of our greatest assignments of all we have done in our lives thus far.

The cruise ship returned safely back to Haifa ten days later, and all the Jewish families were dispersed throughout Israel. A year later, we happened to meet up with a couple of families. I had been asked to lead worship at a center in the Galilee, and just prior to beginning the evening, in walked one of the families that had been on the ship with us! In a joyous reunion, I was stunned to find out that this family had come to faith in Yeshua (Jesus) as their Messiah in the past year there in the Galilee. To me it was a vivid reminder of what God prophetically promised He would do in returning His people to their homeland Israel:

> I will bring My exiled people of Israel back from distant lands [55] . . .

---

[55]   Amos 9:14.

I will plant them in their own Land[56]*. . .*

I will give them a heart to know Me[57]*. . .*

When they seek Me with all of their hearts, they will find Me.[58]

Here was proof of God's heart for the Jewish people. We were firsthand witnesses of the goodness of God towards His people all of the years we had the great privilege to live alongside them. God is indeed good to Israel and will continue to pour out His blessings to them. This fact alone gives us confidence He will be faithful to us as well.

Stay Dressed, Ready for Service

This experience was a real example to live in a "ready" mode. Through our 40 years together, my husband and I have chosen to stay detached from anything that would hinder this readiness or distract or prevent us from being activated into His service at a moment's notice. We are like active soldiers dressed, fully armed, and awaiting our next orders to "ship out." For this reason, whenever we travel, we purposely pack very light. We live uncluttered with a simple lifestyle and travel the same way.

In addition, we intentionally live on the offensive rather than a spiritually defensive stance. It is our preference to live in such a way that our senses will stay acute to perceive the strategies of the Lord to disarm the tactics of the enemy who seeks to kill, destroy, and rob us, our family, or friends. We have

---

[56] Amos 9:15.

[57] Jer. 24:7.

[58] Jer. 29:13.

not always been successful, and at times, even failed, but God's nature is redemptive, and His mercy always seeks our good as His kindness draws us to the place of His greatest blessings.

Since Ron's vision, we made a further decision to maintain a household atmosphere full of His presence, His shalom, super-faith, great joy, and to live without the mind-dulling distraction of entertainment. This creates an environment that maximizes an awakened spirit to perceive the subtle ways the Holy Spirit communicates. We have determined to hear Him and be ready to respond.

Our years living in the unstable conditions of the Middle East taught us that things can change in an instant, and we have been conditioned to live in a state of high alert. From time to time, the Lord has brought this section of Scripture to mind which I believe is a good reminder of how to live as citizens of another Kingdom.

> *Be ready for service and have your lamps lit. You must be like people waiting for their master to return from the wedding banquet so that when he comes and knocks, they can open the door for him at once. Those slaves the master will find alert when he comes will be blessed. I assure you: He will get ready, have them recline at the table, then come and serve them. If he comes in the middle of the night, or even near dawn, and finds them alert, those slaves are blessed. But know this, if the homeowner had known at what hour the thief was coming, he would not have let his house be broken into. You also be ready, because the Son of Man is coming at an hour that you do not expect. (Luke 12:35-40, HCSB)*

While still living in Jerusalem, I remember the day I sensed the Lord telling me, "Go through everything you own." I began to do just that, giving items away and discarding piles of accumulation, but not fully understanding the reason.

About 3 months later I had a questioning time from the Holy Spirit: "If you were given a very short time to leave the country, what would you take? Put those items in a box, and leave them in a closet." This is an exercise I highly recommend. It will help you view your priorities of life. Look around your home and consider what are the items you must have with you at all times? What do you require just to live life? It reveals what we consider important necessities.

I did do this and put all of those items in a dedicated closet for 8 months. It was at that time we received the shocking news that we had 12-days to liquidate our household and leave Israel. Had I not heeded the warning of the Holy Spirit, our departure could have been much more difficult.

I realize that most people are not required to live in this high state of readiness, but it is a good exercise nonetheless and can be a barometer of our heart attachment to material possessions.

Follow the Leader

The main objective is that we remain sensitive to what the Holy Spirit is prompting us to do. We rarely understand the whys in the moment; we only feel the urgency. Only much later can we piece together how God was leading us at the time, even though we did not realize it. The Holy Spirit will train us to recognize when He is prompting us. When you ask Him to do this, you are then much more expectant and aware of His leading.

Before our "Europe: 40-Days-to-Pray" journey, God exercised Ron and I in many ways to sharpen our ability to hear Him, confirm that we heard correctly, and learn to respond without fully understanding with our minds. It is a necessary step to follow His lead without knowing the logic or the reason.

One of the ways He taught us while we were in the USA

was to direct us to go somewhere for a specific mission. We had little notice ahead of time. One of these Holy Spirit mission-training exercises was to pray along the California highway 99 and highway 5 corridors that run the length of the west coast. We had learned, much to our surprise, that Islam has made this particular route an intentional strategy in the USA where they established Islamic communities, centers, and mosques off the beaten path and in very small communities. God would often prompt us to find these and pray there. We always pray that God would give the Muslim community dreams and visions of Jesus of Nazareth. We have done this from Los Angeles all the way into Canada. Our focus, however, was Stockton and Lodi, not far from where we were living while in Northern California, and they were the very first cities where we prayed around mosques.

As we made our Europe prayer tour a couple of years later, God confirmed to us in so many ways that He had led us on this trip and that it would be very fruitful. He always lets us know, with confirmation, that He is leading. While we were in Turkey, the very last leg of nearly 50 days in Europe, God confirmed again that He had indeed led us to pray in this way.

Full Ramadan Moon over Istanbul

We were in Istanbul during the very middle of Ramadan when the moon was full and felt it was strategically important to pray there exactly at that time. The city of Istanbul swells to millions of people from all over the Middle East and Europe because of its spiritual significance and age-old mosques. This ancient city of Constantinople was at one time a highly influential Christian city before it was forced to convert to Islam. At the very far reaches of Europe, Istanbul was indeed a key city in which to conclude our prayer journey.

Ron circled the mosques in a stealth manner at the time of the Islamic evening prayers, anointing the grounds with oil, and praying for God to reveal Jesus of Nazareth through dreams and visions, and with signs and wonders.

The next day as we prayed, we sensed we needed to walk through the ancient Istanbul bazaar with over 3,000 shops. On this prayer journey through Europe, we were purposely not buying souvenirs since we were traveling with only 50 pounds between us. The intention of our visit to the bazaar was to "shop" for treasures of a different kind, people God perfectly arranged for us. We were really looking forward to this adventure!

During our "shopping" spree, we had great opportunities to engage with the Turkish people in the ancient souk. The sights, sounds, and smells had retained a centuries-old authenticity. We came to the end of the marketplace and turned up a street to find the public transport. At that moment, a shopkeeper stepped forward and intercepted us.

"You want to buy carpet?" he asked waving his hand and pointing across the street. "Come to my shop."

"Oh, we are not buying carpets today," Ron answered stepping around him, "but thank you." As we continued up the street, the shopkeeper followed alongside of us.

"I make for you coffee. Come to my shop . . . please," he insisted.

Ron stopped, looked at him intently and asked, "Where did you learn such beautiful English?"

"I worked in America!" he said, squaring his shoulders and smiling proudly.

"Really? Where?" Ron asked. We both realized this could be a God-arranged appointment.

"In California!" our friend answered. Ron and I exchanged glances.

"What? You lived in California? That's where we live. Where in California?" Ron inquired. This carpet seller had our full attention and we leaned in excitedly.

"Well, I lived in Stockton and worked in Lodi."

There it was . . . our confirmation. His response caused us to burst out laughing right there on the street. God really outdoes Himself and will go out of His way to make such connections! Later we considered the amazing events of the day and how God had led us so perfectly to this one man in a huge city with millions of tourists in the middle of Ramadan, intersecting the three of us at that exact moment.

We found out that our Turkish Muslim friend had just returned from the United States where he had been an accountant for a large industrial firm for two years. Ron realized that Ahmad[59] had been in California at the very time when he had brought teams to pray around the mosques of Stockton and Lodi. We were able to pray for him right there on the streets of Istanbul and blessed his family and business. He was so grateful.

God brings encouragement and confirmation in the most stunning ways so there is no doubt in our mind. To us, this was proof that we were at the right place at the right time. Throughout our journey across Europe, we experienced similar confirmations that demonstrated the Holy Spirit was leading us in His perfect way.

Decisions, Decisions

Our "Europe: 40-Days-to-Pray" trip had led us to Paris, where we seemed to be stuck. It was a puzzle and nothing seemed to be working out. We were prayerfully attempting to discern the mind of the Lord in the Paris train station, wondering which direction we should go: east or west? Sometimes attempting to get direction from the Holy Spirit cannot be easily discerned nor does it make logical sense in the moment, especially with the pressure to make an immediate decision. What is needed in

---

[59] Not his real name.

such moments is God's peace with the decision we finally settle on, and then, rest with confidence that He is leading. We felt His peace as we decided to head the complete opposite direction of our planned itinerary, traveling by sleeper train east from Paris all the way to Madrid. It made no sense, but with the presence of His peace, we were full of anticipation.

Andalucía, Spain

Arriving in Spain early in the morning, we were excited to make the route where Islam had crossed over into Spain in the year A.D. 711. The Islamic conquest of Spain and renaming of the nation to "Andalucía" was a dark time for Christianity, and indeed for the continent of Europe. The Islamists had every intention of launching from Spain the full conquest of Europe. They were stopped in Poitiers, France, in A.D. 732, however. The history of how Spain expelled the Islamists from their soil has been a sore spot in Islam ever since. *Once Allah's land, always Allah's land* is more than a motto; it is an Islamic mandate.

Our mandate on this trip was to follow that ancient conquest route by train and bus and declare: "Spain belongs to Jesus." With each train stop along the way, we anointed the ground with oil, made declarations for the spiritual inheritance over the nation of Spain, and prayed for dreams and visions of Jesus of Nazareth in every Muslim community we were able to get to. Along the route, God gave me (Carol) a vision of thousands of Spanish youth set on fire for Jesus igniting a wildfire of passion for Him across Europe. God also gave us a number of people to connect with who became our confirmations of His plan and signs that what we were doing would be fruitful.

We traveled from Madrid to Tarifa, the very tip of southernmost Spain. Spending a couple of nights there allowed us to pray through this strategic and ancient port city and reinforce a spiritual boundary between Islamic North Africa and Christian

Europe. We were declaring in the spirit to Islamic strongholds across the Mediterranean Sea: "You may not enter here again."

Tangier, Morocco

The next day, we took the hydrofoil and disembarked into North Africa at the Port of Tangier. Our arrival came two days earlier than we had originally planned. However, we were in expectation and knew there had to be a stunning reason.

What awaited us was an unusual welcoming committee— business-hungry tour guides. With much effort, we explained that we did not need a tour guide through their city; however, they were undeterred and continued to press us toward their vehicles. We felt strongly that we must first walk on foot through this city to see how God would lead us to pray.

We left the port to the main street trying to sense God's leading. As foreigners, we caught the attention of preying shop owners.

"Halo, Madame!" they called out, rushing out to greet us.

"Come into my shop, sir! You like to buy carpet today?" asking Ron in perfect English. I always marvel at the way shop owners can spot a tourist far away and be able to discern exactly what language he speaks. Surrounded on all sides by crowds of people moving up and down the main street, I felt someone begin to follow us.

"Good morning! You need a guide through Tangier? I help you . . . come with me!" Mohammed urged us to hire him as a personal tour guide, but I sensed an alert in my spirit.

"Oh, thanks very much . . . we do not need a tour guide today!" I told him as we tried to move around him. Mohammed would not give up. He followed us down the street, continuing to urge us. We could see our refusals were not convincing him. Carol had now positioned herself to walk behind me, single file, not so much to adhere to protocol of an Islamic state, but rather as protective intercession. Mohammed continued with every persuasive angle he could think of.

"Where you go today? You cannot find your own way. Impossible! Come, I show you . . . special price for Americans today . . . cheap!" He actually had a very charming character and spoke English surprisingly well. For several blocks our would-be guide followed us, and with each refusal for his services, his responses became increasingly angry and more harassing.

Soon he was joined by another man, much more aggressive. At our persistent refusal to hire him, he became mocking, rude, and surly. We tried to ditch him by slipping into a store to purchase water. When we came out, he simply picked up where he left off.

"Come to my home, I make you coffee, then I show you Tangier . . ." he insisted again.

If I have learned anything the last few years, it is that remaining calm in such situations is important. Each time I tried to politely let him know we were not in need of his services, he became more aggressive. That let me know there was more than meets the eye. This was not just another of the scores who had followed us requesting to be hired; I discerned instead that this was a demonic assignment sent to distract us from what God had for us in the city. We were determined to accomplish Heaven's assignment during our short time in Tangier.

Carol was still behind me and told me later that she sensed in the spirit that he was attempting to rattle me so that I would respond in anger, a typical tactic in Islam, inciting anger to bring confusion. Carol began to speak in heavenly tongues behind me, and not quietly, but out loud . . . loud enough for our angry wannna-be-tour guide to hear. It was directed at the enemy. He whirled around to face her and demanded, "What are you doing?" His angry response was a clue that something was breaking in the spirit realm, so we continued.

It was comical really. We both now were responding to his harassment by speaking in tongues. These men are brilliant in their command of languages because their business demands it. As I spoke in tongues, he attempted to respond to me in several languages: French, Spanish, German and others that I did not recognize. Finally, in a rage, he turned on his heels and headed off in the opposite direction. And with him, the oppressive cloud of confusion he carried. Peace descended, we regained clarity of mind, and continued our walk uphill through the city.

It was about 9:00 in the morning now, and looking at the map, we prayerfully considered where to go in the city. We decided our first stop would be the historical Anglican Church in Tangier. Part of our assignment in Europe was to pray in the ancient churches, to call forth their inheritance and harvest of seed that had been sown through the centuries. We also prayed for revival in these nations.

Oldest Anglican Church in North Africa

Finding the church on our map, we went into the complex through an iron gate which led into a beautiful English garden, typical of Anglican churches. The peace we felt on the grounds was tangible, a stark contrast to the bustle of the Islamic city outside of the walled church grounds. We prayed and rested in the shade of the garden for a few moments and then went into the ancient church.

The inside was shockingly run down, as if it had not been in active use for quite some time. Sadly, it was more like a museum. There was a man inside of whom we inquired about the history of the church. Thinking him to be the Anglican Vicar in charge, we were surprised to learn that he was, in fact, a Muslim! Now we knew we had come to the right place and that we needed to pray and worship there.

While I engaged the man in a warm, friendly conversation, Carol found a dusty Anglican hymnal and began to thumb through it. Soon her voice began to rise and fall, singing out the familiar Anglican melodies from the hymnal. It had probably been quite a few years since this church had any worship whatsoever. It just seemed right that Jesus should be praised in this dilapidated church.

Power of Thanksgiving

As Carol continued singing and worshiping Jesus, strolling up and down its aisles, I began to inquire about the caretaker's health. As the atmosphere of Heaven reverberated against the stone interior and filled the sanctuary once again, God's presence was clearly affecting the man as I spoke to him. I prayed for his shoulder in the name of Jesus, and all the while, his attention was jerked back and forth between my prayer and Carol's singing as God was massaging his heart. As we left the church that day, he appeared dazed by God's presence. We felt like we left this ancient church better than we found it.

A simple conversation and singing a song are not what they appear to be when executed by trained warriors of God's kingdom. At the sound of our voice, God dispatches Heaven's reinforcements to overturn the atmosphere and create favorable conditions for men's hearts to receive His love and mercy. What God has provided for us are powerful weapons in His arsenal to bring the enemy camp to its knees. Love will do this . . . the sound of worship and thanksgiving in any situation will always do this. It is the very weapon with which God sent the Israelites into war . . . the sound of their thanksgiving rising up to Heaven sent confusion into the camp of the enemy, assuring victory.

> Then he consulted with the people and appointed some to sing for the LORD and some to praise the splendor of His holiness.

When they went out in front of the armed forces, they kept singing: Give thanks to the LORD, for His faithful love endures forever."

The moment they began their shouts and praises, the LORD set an ambush against the Ammonites, Moabites, and the inhabitants of Mount Seir who came to fight against Judah, and they were defeated. (2 Chronicles 20:21)

God always sends His people into battle with a secure victory because of His favor on them. In this case, God instructed the armed military to be preceded by a priestly choir and musical instruments. As they sang thanksgiving to God, the battle was won because confusion of the enemy is always the expected result. God always removes their defenses as we worship Him.

Only be not afraid of the people of the land, for we will devour them. Their protection has been removed from them, and the LORD is with us. Don't be afraid of them! (Numbers 14:9)

Only those filled with faith can see right into the enemy's camp at how easily God will bring victory. Whereas those with doubt see only the enemy coming at them and it fills them with dread. Because of his trust in God, God allowed Caleb to see deep into enemy territory and discern that they were defenseless against God with His people. I believe Caleb was shown their debilitating fear that would make the bravest warrior weep knowing what was coming at him. I can just see Caleb transported invisibly before their most powerful men, watching their faces and sensing what was happening in their spirits. The reputation of the Israelites had preceded them, and the news was terrifying. Caleb was confident in God and ready to act upon his vision because he was a man of another spirit.

A Grand Mosque

We moved from the peaceful complex of the church back out onto the bustling streets of Tangier. The oppressive cloud of Islam hung over the city, and its effect was tangible. Since it was Friday, we knew it would soon be time for corporate prayers at the mosque. We looked over our map to decide which mosque we wanted to visit. We decided on the largest one and realized it was just a few short blocks away from where we were.

The heat by 11:00 on this July morning was already intense. We stopped to drink water and headed by foot toward the mosque. We decided that Carol would not walk behind me as is customary for women, but rather, beside me, as a way to prophetically declare Islamic women delivered into freedom.

We spotted the Grand Mosque of Tangier just up ahead, creamy white in typical Moroccan architectural style reaching far above the surrounding buildings. Its dome could clearly be seen, and we walked boldly toward our prayer objective. The small, pocket-sized bottle of anointing oil we carried all through Europe was ready, brimming with a fresh combination of wine and oil, representing joy and healing.

Moving closer to the mosque, we observed the men stationed as guards at the elaborate hand-carved wooden doors. We decided that Carol would stay back and I would circle the mosque, discreetly sprinkling anointing oil on the grounds.

King of Morocco Comes to Town

Completing the circuit and returning to where Carol was waiting, I noticed a white flag flying from the minaret tower where the Islamic call to prayer is sounded. I drew Carol's attention to the flag, "Hey, in London when they fly the white flag, it means the Queen is in residence. I wonder what it could mean here?"

Soon enough we would find out.

As we stood across the street from the entrance of the

mosque, a parade of dignitaries began to arrive in regal Islamic dress. Security officers appeared in black suits and ties, followed by carload after carload of Islamic clerics. It was a red-carpet parade with the common people waving Moroccan flags on the sidelines. Carol was busy taking photos of all the excitement and motorcades of dignitaries.

"Do you know why there are red flags today?" a man standing by asked us. We were even more than curious now.

"No, what is it?" I asked the man.

"The king is inside the mosque today celebrating the birthday of the crown!"

It all began to make sense now! We had seen gigantic red flags flying all over the city from the time we disembarked from the ferry. The capital city of Morocco and actual residence of the king is a few hours southwest of Tangier. And yet, here we were, on Friday, Islamic holy day, on the anniversary of the Crown of Morocco with the king inside the very mosque we had just prayed over, anointed, and circled!

Wow. God's timing amazed us, and with such confirmation again. Now we understood better why we took the train from Paris to Madrid and then felt the urgency to get to Morocco and arrive in Tangier two days earlier than we had originally planned. The king was not there on Thursday, and he would not be there on Saturday. He was only there on the one day we were able to get in and out of Morocco. And this was the very day of God's special appointment to circle the king of Morocco and pray that God would give visions and dreams of Jesus of Nazareth into the heart of this Islamic leader. It excited us with fresh expectation as we considered how perfectly God set this up. These signs from Heaven give you confidence with the unexpected that happens.

Carol and I stood across the street from the main entrance door with a front row view of the Grand Mosque doorway. The time for noon prayers was fast approaching, and with it, a continual stream of cars arrived unloading diplomats, Moroccan government officials, Muslim clerics, and dignitaries in regal dress. Carol was still snapping photo after photo as were many other Moroccans standing around us. This was an unusual and momentous occasion for Tangier. The streets were quite crowded now with thousands of citizens watching the parade. We learned that in the evening there would be a huge celebration marked with parties and fireworks, and we saw the wisdom of the Holy Spirit leading us to stay only one day in Tangier.

All the King's Men

Observing all the excitement, Carol leaned over to me suddenly and asked, "Why is that man waving at me?" I looked at the mosque entrance across the street. Sure enough I could see the black-suited security men looking our direction and gesticulating with their hands in waving motions.

"Seems like he wants me to stop taking photos!" Carol said. She put her camera down, and we resumed watching the parade of Muslim clerics dressed in their long white robes enter the mosque with great ceremony.

"Everyone else is taking photos . . ." Carol said a few minutes later looking around. It was true, people all around us were photographing this royal parade. She resumed taking photos, thinking perhaps it was not her they were signaling. We both continued to snap pictures of arriving clerics and special guests. I had a very small pocket camera which was easily concealed. Her camera, however, was a larger 35-mm. The men-in-black gesticulated in Carol's direction from across the street once again, only with much more intensity. *What could that mean?* we wondered. She continued to take photos assuming it was for someone else.

Suddenly, two of the security guards broke ranks and came rushing in our direction from across the street pushing their way through the crowd. I immediately slipped my little camera into my back pocket. Carol was standing with her camera in hand. Now we knew it was us they were signaling. Carol made an instant decision not to cower in fear, but rather, to walk intentionally towards the fierce-looking security guards rushing at her. I took my place at her side.

"Hi," Carol cheerily greeted the men-in-black with their entourage in tow. "Were you trying to get my attention for some reason?" You might as well be confident in who you are, was her approach. We were tourists, after all.

"Why you take photos?" the king's guard demanded in broken English moving closer to Carol. "It is forbidden!" eyeing her camera suspiciously. His anger was palatable. A crowd began to gather around us, all eyes upon the two Americans being accosted by the king's security detail.

"It is forbidden? Really?" Carol replied. "Because other people here. . ." sweeping her arms wide to the crowd with cameras.

"Forbidden!" he spewed out, his anger clearly rising now at this un-Islamic woman addressing him in such a bold manner. Tapping her camera he demanded, "Take out photos. . . Now!"

"But, there is no film . . . it is digital. I can erase them though," Carol offered in a calm voice, displaying the photos she had taken one by one.

"Ephas!" banging his finger on her camera. *"Ephas!"* he said louder for emphasis. We immediately recognized this Arabic word to mean, "erase it." Compliant, Carol began to delete each photo as the chief for the king's security team viewed each photo pointing and demanding, "Ephas!"

Meanwhile, his second-in-command, towering above everyone around him, stood watching all of this. He occasionally leaned down to comment now and then to his partner in Arabic, and then translated in English to us.

"I'm sorry that you must erase all your photos, but it is

forbidden to photograph the king in the mosque," he politely explained. I was surprised at his perfect English and the contrast of his demeanor.

"We were trying to tell you to stop taking photographs," he went on to say, "because it is forbidden." It sort of seemed like a good-cop, bad-cop-act in a way. We knew there would be no arguing and had resigned ourselves to deleting the photos we had taken the whole morning. With each photo the head of security viewed, the more intense he became, fuming and shooting angry glances at Carol as if she had violated Moroccan policy intentionally. All the while, I had the joyful satisfaction of knowing that I still had photos of our day on my pocket-sized camera safely tucked away.

Carol was handling herself quite well in the face (quite literally) of this angry Moroccan security official. His frustration no doubt may have been that Carol was a woman who refused to cower with fear.

As they continued to scroll one-by-one through the photos on her camera, Mr. Good Cop stepped forward and seemed clearly embarrassed by his partner's intensity. He began to engage us with small talk.

"Where are you from?" he asked me.

"California," I answered. Carol, still deleting photos added, "You know . . . Hollywood!" With that, the crowd around us relaxed and echoed, "Oh . . . Hollywood!"

For us, this was a diversionary moment which we hoped would lighten up the tension. Mr. Bad Cop was now satisfied that all the photos were deleted from the camera and he stepped off to the side, still glaring. I stayed close to Carol's side.

"Yes, Hollywood!" we answered, smiling and laughing. "Have you been to California? You should come!" The tensions were lessening and being displaced by joy.

Mr. Good Cop continued with his friendly exchange, "As the

head of security for the king of Morocco, we want to officially welcome you to our nation!" We shook hands with Mr. Good Cop and his security team, pleased by his friendliness and the official welcome to Morocco by all the king's men.

"We hope you have a nice stay in our country."

"Thank you so much!" I said, my heart still beating fast from this close call. With this, the king's men headed back to the mosque entrance. Mr. Bad Cop turned around, and shaking his finger at Carol gave a final stern warning, "No more photos!"

Carol immediately demonstrated that she was putting her camera into the backpack as we both waved a friendly goodbye. Heading away from the Grand Mosque towards the center of the city, we were both giddy with the joy of the Lord, having received a personal welcome to this Islamic country by the king's men.

Mission accomplished.

Displacing Darkness

Had we not responded to the Holy Spirit's leading back in Paris, we would have missed this momentous occasion of the king in Tangier. God had set it up that we would pray around the largest mosque in Tangier while the king was praying inside. We spent the rest of our day with a very friendly taxi driver who took us to the highest places of the city, giving us a grand prayer tour, and ending at the ancient Jewish synagogue of Tangier.

We believe that our time of praying around the city created a tangible presence of God. That is the power of walking into dark places. We know that we carry God's light, and everywhere we go, His brilliance released will always displace darkness.

Lord of the Harvest

In 1980, we made a 3-month evangelistic outreach trip throughout the UK and Europe and were stunned by the spiritual darkness. In 2010, exactly 30 years later, God arranged for us to return to pray through Europe again for nearly 50 days.

One of the things we prayed in 2010 was that the Lord would send Arabic-speaking leaders and ministries throughout Europe specifically into these Muslim communities.

In 2012, during the Summer Olympics in London, Ron was asked to be a part of an Arabic-speaking outreach there. At that time, he actually met the very ones we had prayed God would send to work there two years earlier, the exact time He had us pray "Lord of the Harvest, send workers!" It is encouraging when you see God answer your prayers so specifically and how His leading is perfectly arranged through amazing circumstances. When we review these experiences, we have hopeful anticipation to trust Him for the very next thing He leads us to do.

God is preparing His willing people who volunteer to stay ready to be deployed. People and nations are depending on us to courageously heed the call of the Lord of the Harvest.

God's Blessing on You

God has determined that we will be blessed as we glorify His name and seek to advance His kingdom. Even in a time of the most distressing circumstances, He is able to bring increase with little and bless every single effort.

> *Isaac sowed seed in that land, and in that year he reaped a hundred times what was sown. The LORD blessed him.* (Genesis 26:12)

We would like to pray a blessing over your life. Though you may have been in a situation where you have been wronged, are in famine conditions, or have experienced distressing life events, we pray this over you now:

> *Father, cause the seed that was sown in good soil to reap a supernatural abundance of one hundredfold. Father, bless and bring increase. For Your glory, Amen.*

Deuteronomy 33:13-16 has had a particular emphasis in our hearts, and we would also like to pray this special prayer of blessing over your life:

> *May the LORD bless his land with the precious dew from heaven above and with the deep waters that lie below; with the best the sun brings forth and the finest the moon can yield; with the choicest gifts of the ancient mountains and the fruitfulness of the everlasting hills; with the best gifts of the earth and its fullness and the favor of him who dwelt in the burning bush.*

> *Father, thank You for Your great favor—"the favor of Him who dwelt in the burning bush"—upon them to fulfill all You have put in their hearts. May its effect be far reaching to expand Your kingdom exponentially. For the glory of Jesus' name, Amen.*

There has never
been a moment when
God diverted
His focused gaze
from you...
not ever.

PRESENCE-DRIVEN

But David strengthened himself in the LORD his God. (2 Samuel 30:6b)

David exemplified a presence-driven life. He turned to the Lord in every situation. He lived as one who relied wholly upon God for salvation, deliverance, and help in times of trouble. God was the source for all he needed. When things went from bad to worse, David knew how to find the Lord and receive strength.

Only a handful of characters in the Old Testament demonstrated such union with the Holy Spirit. When a giant terrified the entire Israeli army, David was not afraid to confront him. With God's affirmation and a single stone, David took him down, immediately releasing courage in the hearts of the soldiers around him and gaining a victory against their Philistine enemy. That was crazy faith in action if we ever saw it.

This is exactly the kind of relationship the Lord desires with each of us—where our dependence upon Him is so real, no giant can stand against us or our family as we walk in His presence. David remains the example of one God refers to as "a man after My own heart,"[60] who from boyhood until his death was marked with the manifest presence of God.

The Strength of His Presence

David knew how to strengthen himself in God when everything and everyone seemed to be against him. In the story of David at Ziklag, his men were ready to stone him. An army had invaded his camp and taken everything away—wives, children, his personal belongings, and all that belonged to his men. In the backdrop of all of this, King Saul had a price on his head and was looking to kill him! Clearly he was not having a good day.

Yet, David had trained himself how to find God and His strength whenever things looked bad. We have to know what that will look like long before we ever come to that place of desperation.

When we are in the midst of the worst times of our lives, we have to know how to find the strength of God's presence when we do not know anything else. It will be different for each one of us. Ask yourself, what posture do I take when I am intentionally seeking God? For me (Carol) personally, I will pull away from my normal activities and anything that distracts in order to take the time to saturate in God's presence and His Word. I focus on tuning in to hear and intentionally listen to what the Holy Spirit is saying to me. Sometimes we can feel overwhelmed with debilitating fear in a situation. Training ourselves to receive from God long before those distressing times are upon us is vital.

---

[60] Acts 13:22.

Seek the Lord while He may be found; call to Him
while He is near. (Isaiah 55:6)

This Scripture is a strong, urgent call from the Holy Spirit. God gives us seasons when everything is going well. It is in those times that we are able to pursue Him for a deeper relationship and take care not to neglect deep communion with Him. These are the times when it is easier to find His presence and receive revelation of His character and nature that sustain and strengthen us. The "easy" times are often preparation for the unforeseen difficulties just ahead. It is in the quiet, peaceful times when we are built up, strengthened, and equipped with tools that help us to endure any battle as we are exercised to live in God's rest and peace.

In our busiest, distressing, and most stressful times, we must also find ways to take breaks through it all, allowing God's presence and His Word to penetrate the tension with His reality and truth. When we do this, we will find God's proper perspective as He breathes the fresh air of Heaven's wisdom upon us. We will always be strengthened and empowered as we encounter God's presence with us, no matter how desperate our situation.

David knew how to do this. In this situation, God gave him the exact strategy on how to get back everything that was stolen at Ziklag. Little did he know that God was also setting up his royal rule. Simultaneous to his recovery operation, King Saul and his son Jonathan were killed in battle, immediately making David the *de facto* ruler of the kingdom. His not-so-good day ended up to be his best day ever.

A Rabbi's Blessing

I (Carol) remember a particularly difficult time in Jerusalem with the mounting pressures of life and doubt concerning the effectiveness of my ministry. Sometimes you just wonder if what you are doing is productive.

One day I was waiting for the bus in my neighborhood to take me to the convention center where I would be leading worship that night. Feeling a bit downcast and standing apart from the gathering crowd, I was quietly communing with the Lord. Out of nowhere it seemed, a very elderly, white haired, ultra-Orthodox Jewish man dressed in all black, made his way slowly toward the bus stop. With halting steps he scanned the crowd and then came directly toward me.

I shifted my heavy guitar to the other hand, curious about this elderly gentleman I had never seen in my neighborhood before. *He must be a visiting rabbi*, I thought.

The elderly man walked over to me, stopped, pointed up to the sky, and then began to sing the Aaronic benediction in Hebrew. I'm sure my mouth was gaping open in surprise, and I suddenly realized all the people at my bus stop were staring my direction.

"The LORD bless you, the Lord keep you . . .," the Rabbi sang out in Hebrew. "May the LORD make His face shine upon you and be gracious to you," his voice rising and falling with the ancient Hebrew melody. In the distance, I could hear bus number 7 round the corner and make its way down the hill to my stop as the rabbi continued to gesticulate heavenward as he sang the ancient priestly blessing.

"The LORD lift up His face and give you shalom," his voice rang out. When he finished, I thanked him profusely, puzzling over his personal attention, and with his eyes closed he nodded up and down with a smile of satisfaction. I gathered my belongings, picked up my guitar, and moved toward the opened bus door. As one of the last ones to board, I handed my shekels to the driver and made my way through the crowded center aisle. The bus gave a jerk as it started down the street, and I grabbed the bar to steady myself as I stood in the aisle. Shifting my heavy guitar to the other hand, I turned behind me wanting to speak more to the rabbi. To my surprise, he was not there. Grabbing hold of the seat in front of me, I leaned down to look out the window as the bus turned the corner to see if the rabbi was walking on the sidewalk, but he was not. I looked up and down on both sides of the street, but he was nowhere in sight. *How odd. He was not able to walk that fast. . . Where did he go?*

The strange thing is, I never saw this mysterious rabbi again in our neighborhood, and we lived there sixteen years.

I finally came to realize that God had sent encouragement that day to remind me that His presence and the blessing of His name is always on me, no matter how I feel about myself.

We never really know what God is doing behind the scenes as we keep our eyes fixed upon Him in the midst of life's stresses. I will say, from my own experiences, that we can always be assured He is working all things out in our favor and setting up circumstances that will work for us, not against us.

Fervent Genuine Worship

The fervent lifestyle of a worshiper cannot be contained within the confines of religious forms. It must have freedom of expression! It is interesting to note that all revivalists and reformers went outside of the standard behavior that was considered "normal" in their day. A presence-driven worshiper cannot adhere to the status quo and must live outside the "box."

The startling result of living with the reality of God's presence on us is the transforming atmosphere wherever we are. When a person knows that God is with him and that God's favor is on him, he walks in an extreme faith that is not of this world. He also releases an environment of transformation and freedom without even trying.

To some, this fervent worshiper with his freedom of expression may be labeled "crazy." Whatever Kingdom task these worshipers do seems "over-the-top."

Our mandate is to create this atmosphere, an environment of God's manifest presence wherever we are so that people can encounter the living God, be impacted and forever changed by Him. As ones filled with the Spirit of God, we are the temple of His presence on the earth, and sometimes our genuine worship and fervent responses will look a little crazy, perhaps even extreme. Yet, our fervent love expressed will be a testimony to those who do not know God as Father and have never personally experienced His love.

Muslim Work Crew

I (Ron) had hired a crew of gardeners to landscape the backyard of the ministry building where we worked in Jerusalem. Though Atef and his crew were practicing Muslims, a friendship developed over several months. I often visited Atef in his village where the family fixed me dinner and sent home freshly made sheep cheese. Every day I was out working alongside of them, which often led to interesting discussions contrasting our two faiths.

One day, while the crew worked in the garden, I led worship with my guitar for the ministry staff in the offices upstairs. The joyous songs and music flowed from the open window out to the garden. Afterward, I joined Atef and his crew outside for tea.

"Ron, what were you all doing up there . . . the music, the singing . . . what was that?" Atef asked, handing me a cup of hot mint tea. I thought carefully how to communicate to my Muslim friend the distinctions between Christian worship and Islamic worship.

"Out of deep gratitude," I explained, "we Christians sing songs to God our heavenly Father as a way to express our love and worship."

I (Carol) often recall this incident to illustrate how our intimate worship as Christians distinguishes us from other religions. Our loving Father in Heaven desires intimate communion and fellowship. Whereas, the Qur'an[61] offers no such example.

A number of things happen when people experience Father's loving presence for the first time. They often are unable to articulate what it is they are feeling or experiencing except perhaps by their emotions. For many people, emotions are scary, and they do not know how to intellectually interpret them. But the fact is, when we encounter God, our whole person is greatly affected: body, soul, and spirit.

Atef and his workers encountered Father's love through worship. Though they could not understand it by intellectual reasoning, they perceived Father's love for them. This created many opportunities for them to discover more about Father in Heaven as the friendship developed.

Recognizing His Presence

We have experienced that people who do not know the Lord and encounter God in worship do not have religious language for what they are experiencing. They simply know God is in the room, and they feel Him. We have also discovered that people recognize God's presence manifested and can distinguish it from religious hype. People just know when something is real and when something is put on.

One thing I learned as we have worked with Jewish people for over 40 years is that God has put deep within their core the

---

[61] The Qur'an is the Islamic holy book.

ability to recognize His genuine presence. I believe He did this knowing they would be dispersed throughout the world far away from the sanctuary of His Temple.

At our church in Northern California a couple of years ago, a Jewish woman visited with her Jewish friend who is a believer in Jesus. During the worship the newcomer was simply overcome by God's presence. In talking to her after the service and sharing Messiah's love with her, this Jewish woman prayed with me to dedicate her heart to Him. She clearly recognized God was present and wanted Him. To experience God's presence in such a tangible way bypasses all intellectual arguments and reasonings. His presence is all the proof we need.

As I have led worship throughout the world in Jewish communities singing their ancient prayers in Hebrew, I have seen God manifest His presence, and they recognize Him. It may have something to do with the ancient language of Hebrew revived within the last century. The fact is, more Jewish people have experienced their Messiah as I sang and worshiped than any that I have spoken to personally or tried to convince with reasoning. As I sing the familiar Hebrew prayers from the Scriptures, the response of Jewish people is remarkable. It is as if something familiar resonates in their soul, and they cannot help but respond to its sound. Most often they respond with weeping or will be almost frozen in their seats. They always sing along with me and spontaneously celebrate with traditional Israeli dancing.

Joy Explosion

We told the story earlier of the ship that went to Odessa to bring home to Israel several hundred Russian Jews. The night before we were to land in the Port of Haifa, the Israeli diplomatic team came to me (Carol) and asked if I would give a special music concert to the Jewish immigrants. It was our last evening on board all together.

The immigrants had endured months and months of extreme conditions and pressures because of their official request to leave the Ukraine and immigrate to Israel. Persecution of the Jewish communities had been severe with pogroms for over a hundred years. In the 1970s when the Russian Jewish "refuseniks"[62] were forbidden to leave the country, many of them lost their jobs, were denied university training, and many more were imprisoned or exiled to Siberia. Living in Israel at the time allowed us the privilege of traveling to the Ukraine to bring them home.

As the Russian Jews were brought on board our ship, their sadness and grief was tangible, their hearts heavy. How I longed for God to bring them peace and healing from the severe persecution they suffered in life under communism. Oppression and sorrow marked each face.

I remember going to my room and falling face down before the Lord praying, "God, anyone can lead camp songs. I know their Hebrew songs, but I want Your presence in our midst . . . let them sense You with us as I sing their prayers over them." As I read the Bible later on, I took courage with this Scripture:

> You have turned for me my mourning into dancing; You have put off my sackcloth and clothed me with gladness. (Psalm 30:11, NKJV)

Several hundred immigrants gathered the last evening for my concert, along with the Christian team, Israeli diplomats, IDF Special Forces, and the Greek ship crew. I began to sing the familiar ancient Hebrew prayers. Many of the immigrants had their heads bowed down, a clear

---

62 "Refuseniks" was an unofficial term used by the Soviets for individuals who wanted to emigrate out of the former Soviet Union and Eastern Bloc countries but were denied permission.

sign of mourning their past and anxiousness about the future. By the second song, however, they began to glance up at me occasionally. As a worship leader, I am always conscious of what God is doing in the spirit realm, and I sensed He was hovering over them. I felt an expectancy as I began to sense changes in the atmosphere because He was present.

Suddenly, as I was celebrating a lively Hebrew song from the Psalms, joy simply exploded in the room. One of the immigrants who had literally been carried onto the ship weeping and wailing just 4 days earlier, leaped up on her feet and began to spontaneously dance. Several of the Israeli diplomats immediately joined her in a traditional Jewish circle dance. Ron and several Christian workers also joined the circle.

There it is! I thought, *God is removing their sorrow and mourning and turning it to dancing . . . just like He said He would do!*

Joy had broken through the mourning, peace was released, and their gladness could not be contained. The atmosphere completely changed to celebration after that. Each one of those immigrants threw kisses and waved me goodbye at the end of the concert.

God had indeed exchanged their sadness and grief for joy and strengthened their weary souls as He carried them back to their ancestral home of Israel.

Singing over Holocaust Survivors

One of the most significant experiences I had in Jerusalem during my twenty years there was the opportunity to sing for Holocaust survivors. A Christian ministry sponsored a special event and invited over 100 Holocaust survivors who were well into their 80s. They lovingly served a banquet meal, presented gifts, and prepared a wonderful program of comfort—a simple demonstration of love and care from Christian friends.

This ministry had asked me to sing over them. The songs I chose were Hebrew Scripture prayers, ones they knew by heart since they were children. As I sang, the survivors began to weep. At this point I did not want to stand on the stage any longer; I wanted to be down with these dear ones. I moved from the stage and walked among them as I quietly strummed my guitar and sang over them, touching one here, and another there. This personal connection created an environment for God's presence with the wonder of His transformational, healing love. It gave me great satisfaction to sense His Spirit of Comfort present to touch the trauma of their souls, heal the deep wounds of their hearts, and establish His shalom over them.

As I sang, I sensed that for this reason I was born.

Comforting Those Who Mourn

In Jerusalem during a week of nearly daily bus bombings, I had been invited by a large Christian ministry based in Jerusalem to do a special evening for Israeli guests. This event was at the International Convention Center in Jerusalem that held a few thousand people, and the place was packed with Christians and Israeli Jews.

I had a most difficult task to lead songs that would be comforting in nature for this mixed crowd. Because of another terrorist bus bombing just that morning, the entire nation was mourning those who had died. I chose a song from the Psalms which communicated the worshiper's desire for God's love and hope. As the meeting came to a close, my voice rang out the comforting words of the psalmist, a lifeline of hope. One by one Israelis got up from their seats and began to make their way to the stage where I stood singing. As they looked up into my face, tears streaming down their faces, I felt their hearts plead with God for the truth of what I was singing. It was as if the anchor of my soul became a place of safety for each of them. My worship had created an atmosphere for them to experience God's secure presence and drink deep from His well of hope.

Joyful Presence

It is a fact that we are drawn to happy people. Unfortunately, joy has not been the primary characteristic of the Church! I see God changing that, displacing our misery with His joy. The reality is, we Christians have every reason to be demonstrating to the world that we are the happiest people on the planet! He provides and satisfies everything we could ever desire. His joy in us radiates around us and it is what draws people to Jesus.

Taxi Ride through Cairo, Egypt

We had the most amazing and exciting day visiting historical places in Giza, a suburb of Cairo and site of the ancient pyramids. Following that, we spent hours in a 24/7 prayer room in the center of Cairo, and then visited one of the churches where a wedding was in progress with lots of Egyptian celebrative, infectious joy.

After the wedding, we stood in the street for the longest time trying to hail down a taxi as the joy of the Lord, still on us, overflowed. Taxi after taxi passed us by, but it did not diminish our joy level!

Finally, after about a half an hour, a taxi pulled over to drop people off, and we negotiated a ride with him to our destination. Settling on a price, we all piled into the car, Ron in the front with the driver, me and our Egyptian friend in the backseat, joy bubbling over from the events of our day. Our taxi driver eyed each of us curiously as we began to draw him into our conversation. Joy is contagious, and our driver was getting a good dose of it. He began to smile and laugh along with us.

"Are you Christians?" he asked glancing over at Ron sitting next to him. This was an unusual question to ask in a Islamic country, but then, it was obvious that we were American tourists.

"Yes, we are," we answered in unison which set us off in another wave of joyous hilarity. I happened to notice that our driver had tears rolling down his cheeks, so I began to inquire more about him.

"Just this morning," he said, "I prayed and asked God to send someone to encourage me. He answered my prayer! He heard me! He sent you three!"

With this, all four of us laughed at the perfect God-setup to end our perfect day. I began to wonder about our driver's ability to navigate through crazy Cairo night traffic with his eyes blinded by tears. Come to find out, our new Egyptian friend was a Coptic Christian but he had never given his life personally to Jesus.

"Would you like to have this kind of joy, all the time?" Ron asked through our interpreter. He could only nod because his emotions were spilling over. Right there in the taxi, and through copious tears, this man prayed to dedicate his life to Jesus. Afterward, he fairly exploded in the same joy we were experiencing. He could hardly keep his eyes on the road, which was a bit unnerving in Cairo traffic! A few times he broke out in spontaneous praise to God and began to sing his favorite Coptic hymn. All the way to our destination in Giza, he thanked us and expressed gratitude to God for sending us to him.

He did not even charge us for the taxi ride and voiced his sadness that our journey together had ended. As we got out of the taxi, he reached into his top pocket and handed Ron his pack of cigarettes, saying, "Here, I won't need these anymore." God had delivered him of smoking right there! We burst out laughing again and left him joyfully praising Jesus with tears streaming down his face as we waved goodbye.

The most powerful expression of our love for Jesus is simply living the joy that He promised would mark our lives. It is the outworking of His presence in us and on us which we release wherever we go. The result is that people taste and see that the Lord is good . . . He is so good.

Festival of No Kvetching!

The most joyous festival of all the biblical feasts is the Feast of Tabernacles, or Sukkot as it is known in Hebrew. It is a 7-day pilgrimage feast where the Israelites go up to Jerusalem and bring a generous offering. But the most significant feature of this particular holy day is that God commanded it to be a 7-day joy fest! For seven days, there would be no sadness, sorrow, or mourning, only joy . . . lots of celebrative joy!

Ron and I loved this idea so much we began to adopt it as a lifestyle.

The Yiddish word for "complaining" and whining is *kvetch*. It means someone who is an incessant negative, complaining whiner! A few years ago, I (Carol) put out a 7-day "no kvetching" challenge to family and friends. The idea behind this is that there be no complaining about anything or anyone for any reason! It gives everyone a chance to change the bad habit of being focused on negatives throughout the day. It is harder than it seems but so worthwhile to adopt as a lifestyle. The negative is exchanged for thanksgiving, which is the healthier heart attitude to express throughout the day. A thankful heart is a cheerful one and that leads to joy and healing.

> *A cheerful heart is good medicine* . . . (Proverbs 17:22)

I challenge you to try it for a day, seven days, a month, then go ahead and make it a lifestyle. Everyone around you will be so glad you did!

"Stronghold" of Joy

Ron and I love the description in the book of Nehemiah about joy. In this passage, the Jewish exiles had returned from Babylon and were gathered in Jerusalem, most likely, for the joyous harvest Feast of Sukkot. Together they read aloud from God's Word when, suddenly and spontaneously, the congregation began to weep and mourn at the remembrance of their sins that had sent them into exile. But Nehemiah stops them and commands them to celebrate all God has done for them instead. Finally Nehemiah calls out:

> *Do not grieve, because the joy of the LORD is your stronghold.* (Nehemiah 8:10b)

This is not ordinary joy. It is the supernatural joy of His presence that becomes our stronghold, a place of refuge and safety for us. The revelation of the Lord is that the time of mourning and grieving about our past mistakes and sins is done! The blood of Jesus has cleansed and restored us, and we are no longer in exile. The joy, that the Lord provides for us, actually strengthens us body, soul, and spirit. Let us determine to live within the stronghold of joy, and let that be our continual life source and the place where we draw strength and encouragement.

A Presence-Driven Life

Both Carol and I owe our passion for the Jewish people to one beautiful man named Abe Schneider. Abe had a broadcast on Christian radio everyday, and as brand new believers in 1970, neither of us could miss his teachings. This Jewish man with a heart after God, became our mentor. We went often to his ministry offices in Los Angeles, California, and accompanied him for field training as he shared Messiah with his Jewish neighbors. This was before we even met one another.

Abe was one of God's rare jewels. He was a true warrior, presence-driven, yoked to the fire of the Almighty, who literally lost everything to follow Jesus—wife, sons, brothers, mother and father. They all turned against him when he committed his heart to the Messiah and was baptized. But Abe found Jesus more worthy than anything this world could offer. Though he lived alone the rest of his life, he was "glued" to God.

This man was unconcerned about his dignity and lived crazy-in-love with his Messiah doing the craziest things. He went after his Jewish brothers with God's love and a zeal we have yet to see equaled. I believe that Abe helped to birth the present Messianic movement of Jewish believers in the Spirit. From 2:00 to 4:00 AM every morning, he circled the 20th floor of the radio studio, lost in the presence of Jesus and crying out to God on behalf of his city, especially the Jewish community. He would often pull up a chair for Jesus, serve Him tea, and read His Book to Him. Jesus was his best friend and life-long companion.

Abe was our spiritual father, and his testimony and wholehearted devotion to Jesus set the course for our lives. As a Jewish man who loved his people, Abe imparted this deep love within us so that we helped carry on his mandate for the next 35 years.

Abe was terribly persecuted by the Jewish community. He did not hide his faith in any way nor was he ashamed of the Gospel of Jesus. In order to be in the midst of his Jewish brethren, he rented a storefront shop in the heart of the Jewish community in Los Angeles. Often radical Jewish groups would break his front windows, doing damage to his offices. The joy of his heart and the smile on his face never dissipated through all of these trials. We can truly say that he was the happiest man we ever met. Every day Abe went door-to-door in the Jewish residential district imploring his brothers to pray to the God of Abraham, Isaac, and Jacob to reveal the Messiah.

"Just ask God to show you if Yeshua is the Messiah of Israel," Abe would say, "He will!" Scores of people prayed with him, but most spat upon him, cursed him, hit him, or slammed their front door in his face. He loved his people and covered the city in outreach for about 30 years. Carol and I accompanied him many times to visit his neighbors. We spent Friday nights around his dinner table eating bowls of fresh-made borscht, hearing his miraculous testimonies and supernatural exploits for the Kingdom. His life became our standard of commitment of service to Jesus.

When Abe died, thousands filled The Church of the Open Door to celebrate his coronation. He is dancing in Heaven with his Messiah now, the burning love of his life.

Abe never had a church, never even had a Bible study. The only channel out of his secret place with the Father was his daily Christian radio broadcast. Abe was one who hosted the manifest presence of God and walked in the power and joy of the Holy Spirit everywhere he went.

God put the Jewish people deep in our hearts back in 1970 through Abe, allowed us to work alongside of him while he was alive, and then gave us the great privilege to help carry on his ministry work in Los Angeles after he graduated to Heaven.

Shortly thereafter, we were launched to the Middle East.

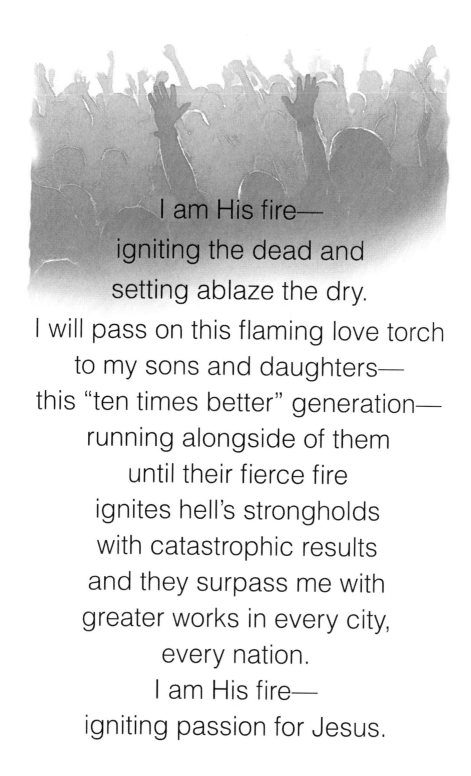

I am His fire—
igniting the dead and
setting ablaze the dry.
I will pass on this flaming love torch
to my sons and daughters—
this "ten times better" generation—
running alongside of them
until their fierce fire
ignites hell's strongholds
with catastrophic results
and they surpass me with
greater works in every city,
every nation.
I am His fire—
igniting passion for Jesus.

TEN

JESUS PEOPLE
TO JESUS CULTURE

W e both came to faith through the Jesus People Movement over 40 years ago, which at the time was moving on the fringe of the predominant Christian denominations and independent churches. Since that time, many groups, ministry organizations, and denominations evolved and small revivals were spawned that have had international impact. We believe that God is moving His Body towards a more all-inclusive Jesus culture. According to Bill Johnson of Bethel Church in Redding, California, we are actually building a "Kingdom culture," where we share "a system of beliefs, disciplines, practices, and relational boundaries that reveal how life is lived among a particular group of people. Movements . . . revivals . . . succeed when they have created a culture that can sustain it."[63] The emphasis will be more on Kingdom relationships and less on that which separates us.

The very week after God hijacked me for His kingdom and thrust me into the Jesus People Movement, I (Ron) revisited a high hill in La Habra Heights, California. This is where I used to go to get high on marijuana, but this time, I was clean. Heaven's atmosphere was all around me, and I found God's presence much more thrilling than any drug I had ever taken.

Sitting there, drinking in God's glory as I stared into the beautiful starry night sky, such an amazing other-worldly peace surrounded me. Worship and gratitude filled my soul in a heart-to-heart exchange with my God. In this high place, I scanned the southern California city of La Habra below me with its lights disappearing to the horizon where the ocean lay. Suddenly, I began to see what I thought were real fires breaking out in the city. Soon there were too many of them to be real and I realized I was seeing a vision.

Then God spoke to my heart, "You will be a participant in setting blazes that will bring My kingdom to Earth." At these words my soul soared with glorious expectations of the future that lay ahead of me. For years I held this pivotal moment in my heart and from time to time reflected on the truth of those prophetic words. As a new believer, I really had no clue how that would come to pass. Looking back over the past 40 years, Carol and I have indeed been setting fires around the world. It has been a remarkable journey for us both, and even now as we have relocated to live in Egypt, we realize it is far from finished.

In the year 2009, I received an upgrade of the vision from La Habra. It seems God waited until I had 36 years of ministry experience coupled with a heart that was transformed into one of furious hunger for more of Him and His glory in the earth.

---

[63] Bill Johnson website: www.bjm.org, "Building A Kingdom Culture."

My eyes are being healed with heavenly eye salve, and my ears are attuned to hear what the Spirit is saying to His church. With this kind of heart that is captivated with God's love in rapt attention, God downloaded what He is about to do in the Church—the "greater" is about to come. The revival we have all cried out for in prayer meeting after prayer meeting is already here, and God is giving us the opportunity to be a part of it. I see this as a progress from one revolution right into the next one: from Jesus people to Jesus culture. Indeed, this generation is living Jesus naturally outside the confines of just doing church, where Jesus is their culture and He goes everywhere they go. This Jesus culture seeks to demonstrate who He is through acts of compassion, especially through the gift of healing. The mandate is:

> *He was moved with compassion for them, and healed their sick.* (Matthew 14:14)

It is the kind nature of the Father being released into the world. He has been waiting for a generation who will demonstrate His heart of compassion where everyone tastes Heaven and gets healed.

The following word came from one of those "grab-your-pen-and-paper-and-take-dictation" moments as I was before the Lord one day. The atmosphere was electric with expectation. Once again, all I could do was write as quickly as I could take the sentences down. And marvel—just marvel!—at what Heaven is releasing in our day.

The Coming Revolution

I am now stacking wood on bonfires throughout the world. The wood that will ignite with My fire is:

- Outcries from My people for more of Me.

- Cries for healing the sick, lame, and blind.
- Cries as intercessors walk the streets of their neighborhoods pleading for revival.
- Cries for outpouring so powerful that people will be seen running into churches from the streets.
- Cries for new fire that will eclipse past revivals and yet stand upon the very foundations that those pillars of the faith laid down long ago.

Soon My Spirit will ignite those dry wood piles of holy expectation. The wave of fire will be catastrophic to sellers of sin. The wave will engulf nations. Rival gods will tremble, burn and sink—sinking into degradation and humiliation as their captives shout out, "I am free!" Proclamations of freedom will continue to fuel that fire which will change history, economies, nations, and peoples. A new mindset will overwhelm My people—a mind that can finally comprehend Me, eyes that can finally see Me, hands that can literally feel My power.

Healing will flow free. My words, "Go and sin no more—" will finally be understood, not as a warning, but as a powerful inoculation against the magnetic drawing power of wickedness. God's saints will walk in power never known before. Men will deliver guilty sinners by the cleanness of their own hands, riches will be weighed out in a new balance.

Assign your nuggets to the dust, your gold of Ophir to the rocks in the ravines—then the Almighty will be your gold and choice silver . . .What you say will be done, and light will shine upon your path . . .When men are brought low, you will say, "Lift them up!" Then He will save the downcast. He will deliver one who is not innocent through the cleanness of your hands.' [64]

---

[64]   Job 22:21-30.

Fearless men and women of God will merely touch the fearful with impartation and boldness from Heaven. Favor will cover My people so strongly that men will be drawn to them.

Life will be brighter than noonday, darkness will become like morning, you will be secure, because there is hope, you will look about and take rest in safety, you will lie down and no one will make you afraid, many will court your favor.' [65]

My love will become tangible. Previous manifestations will have been mile markers to this goal. You will see My love; you will smell My love; you will taste My love.

Old men will rise Caleb-like to take their promised mountains. Women will lead Deborah-like to see into the secret chambers of the enemy.[66] Young men will battle Joshua-like to fell walls of mighty strongholds.

Fear will become a curious memory.

Healing will become commonplace.

Satan's supply line of warehouses to demonic forces deep behind enemy lines will be ransacked by the saints. Those supplies being:

- **Courage**: Intimidation will be changed to courage.
- **Healing**: Sickness will be bound and healed; men's very bones will become life-surging health factories.
- **Faith and trust in God**: Fear will be mocked as the greatest lie.
- **Power**: Timidity will melt like spring snow.
- **Authority**: The least of God's saints will realize that all power belongs to the Lover of their souls who

---

[65] Job 11:19, NIV.

[66] Judg. 5.

freely dispensed God's authority centuries ago to His followers.[67]

- **Love**: Love will impact the body of believers, wiping out the fruits of satan's evil spirit; backbiting, gossip, tale bearing, depression, anger, rage, harshness, pride, aloofness, jealousy, self-serving—all will evaporate in character-transforming, powerful love.

- **Deliverance**: Captives will be loosed, and long-time captives will cry with joy at such victory.

Special forces of the Host of Heaven have been dispatched to lead this new generation to the real power source. Miracles accompany them.

The sticks of wood are like those that healed the bitter, poisoned waters of Marah during the Exodus of the Israelites. Whole cities will become clean and fresh and livable again where once they had been polluted.

My eyes still range throughout the earth to strengthen those whose hearts are fully committed to Me.[68]

Be strong and of good courage![69]

More than Revival

There have been times when Christians have told me that they are weary of hearing about revival but not seeing revival. We can actually be praying for revival and yet miss it because we expect God to move within the confines of a previous move or from our own paradigm. Rarely does that happen. We can also be so community-focused within our own culture circles that we completely miss the fact that God's Spirit has been released in a significant way outside or in another part of the world. What

---

[67] Lk. 10:19, 2 Cor. 10:4.

[68] 2 Chron. 16:9.

[69] Josh. 1:6.

we have found in our travels is that the Church in one region is often not aware of what God is doing elsewhere.

I believe He is about to do much more than revive His people. This concept of revival has the understanding of firing something up that had been dormant, bringing to life something that had been asleep. But, what God is doing is so much greater, the Church cannot contain it! It is something so new it will not fit within the narrow limitations of anything we have known thus far.

The day is coming, and I believe is already here, when crying out for the habitation of His presence is all we can do. We will never again be satisfied with just a visitation of the Spirit of God as with previous revivals which we know only died out later on. No, in our day, He is increasing our capacity to carry His presence and is releasing greater measures of His supernatural power through us and affecting and influencing all spheres of society. I believe this best describes the Jesus culture movement we are presently experiencing and now see growing around the world.

Exploits and Greater Works

There is a generation coming whose lives will be crazier than anything we have yet to see. Their faith will be on the level of "super" that will have the power and proof to release breakthroughs in every nation. No doubt you believe that we are living in the times that Daniel spoke about. It is interesting to consider the "spiritual" environment of Daniel and his friends. At a young age, they were conscripted into the service of the king and constricted by the paranormal Near Eastern religious ritual rites of the Babylonians. They had to be experts in divination and all of the ways of the Babylonian pantheon of gods with its idolatrous sacred worship practices, even though it was forbidden and contrary to their Jewish laws. It did not mean they exercised demonic witchcraft, but they had to know all about it. They were educated in all the sciences and schooled with the finest experts of their day.

But God had a surprise for the Babylonians. With all of their preternatural eastern wisdom, they were no match for the Jewish teenage boys[70] who received downloads of heavenly wisdom and never compromised truth. These young Jewish men actually had to more-than-match the best of those "wise" men.

> In every matter of wisdom and understanding that the king consulted them about [Daniel, Hananiah, Mishael and Azariah], he found them 10 times better than all the diviner-priests and mediums in his entire kingdom. (Daniel 1:20)

God made these young men "ten times better" through the Holy Spirit's supernatural gifts surpassing the idolatrous demon-worshiping priests who manifested satan through witchcraft. These four were the real wise men of the East. In addition, God filled them with Heaven's wisdom and understanding. Their power was unequalled in all of the Babylonian empire.

Yet, Daniel looked ahead and spoke of the generation coming in our day:

> But the people who know[71] their God will be strong and do exploits. Those who are wise among the people will give understanding to many. (Daniel 11:32b, 33a)

Those who walk in such an intimate relationship with God, will know the strength of His power, and supernatural abilities

---

[70] Daniel and his friends may have been around 14 years of age.

[71] The Hebrew word used here for "know" is *yada*, the same word used to describe intimate relations between a man and woman.

will flow out naturally and powerfully through everything they do. Wisdom from the Spirit of God will also flow supernaturally through these presence-driven radical lovers as it did Daniel. Jesus spoke of the ones who will actually have the crazy faith to believe they can work greater miracles than He did.

Greater works than these will you do. (John 14:12)

This is undoubtedly the "Ten-Times Better" generation—the ones who are taking us to the finish line. This generation will shock the world with supernatural wisdom, stunning miracles, signs, and wonders such as we have never before seen as they advance the Kingdom. They will influence every sphere of society as Daniel did. As fathers and mothers of the Church, we have the privilege to encourage and train this Jesus culture, ten-times greater, supernaturally-empowered, warrior generation, so let's do our job well.

The fact is, the world is already being turned upside down in so many places with stunning, powerful demonstrations of Father's love. Both young and old are hitting the streets, schools, and marketplaces living Jesus in supernatural ways.

The promise of dawn is seen, but not yet fully understood.

A Supernatural Culture

The ancient Babylonian and Egyptian civilizations have a history of being spiritually "wise," highly educated, culturally rich, and religiously diverse, as they worshiped a pantheon of gods with magical powers. The Holy Spirit-empowered prophets were sent to these "wise" men with Heaven's signs, wonders, and miracles and were unmatched for anything the demonic powers demonstrated. Why did God do this? Because He loved the people of these nations. Even though these civilizations later became Islamic, the culture of the supernatural is still there, and the history of what God did in their midst is recorded.

For twenty years, Ron and I lived and ministered in Israel. We were eyewitnesses to see God do many things there that could only be attributed to His supernatural works. There are books written by Israelis, for instance, with personal testimonies about what happened during wars as they faced incalculable odds.

We are seeing evidence of the veil being removed from eyes as we hear more and more testimonies of the Son of God being revealed to the people of the Middle East in supernatural ways. It is remarkable to hear testimonies of both Israeli Jews and former Muslims who experience the Messiah through an encounter of the supernatural kind. Because they are reborn in such a way, they minister to other people with the same expectation that God will manifest Himself supernaturally through them. We have heard these testimonies again and again.

We firmly believe that in the nations of the earth, especially Islamic countries, Jesus will be known by the power and demonstration of the Spirit of God through His supernatural gifts. This is already happening. These nations will not have the veil removed from their spiritual eyes because they are convinced intellectually about the deity of the Son of God. Rather, it will be when the Messiah is revealed powerfully in signs, wonders, dreams and visions, through supernatural interventions through His Church that we will see an unparalleled move of God in the Jewish, Islamic, and Arabic-speaking peoples throughout the world.

> *You performed signs and wonders in the land of Egypt and do so to this very day both in Israel and among mankind. You made a name for Yourself, as is the case today.* (Jeremiah 32:20, HCSB)

God is revealing Himself supernaturally in great power to the peoples of this region, but we will see even greater numbers—of biblical proportions!—in the days just ahead.

Fill up their Hands

Before we went to Egypt the first time, God gave me (Ron) a directive for teaching the supernatural gifts of the Holy Spirit, particularly healing. Moses called Aaron and his sons to dress them gloriously, appointing and consecrating them for priesthood.

> *Make tunics, sashes, headbands for Aaron's sons to give them glory and beauty. Put these on your brother Aaron and his sons; then anoint, ordain, and consecrate them, so that they may serve Me as priests.* (Exodus 28:40-41, HCSB)

I always like to check the original words when I run across a phrase that might hold a deeper meaning. I discovered that the Hebrew word for "consecrate" literally says to "fill up their hands." What a word picture; what a concept. I have learned it is the same in Arabic. As Christians, we too, are consecrated priests. With this picture, I was anxious to pray for others to receive this priestly impartation of God's gifts, to "fill up their hands" for ministry.

For too long we have been under the incorrect assumption that the gift of healing, the gift of prophesy, or gift of the word of knowledge were for only a select few. These "gifted" people go to the nations and they are often treated like superstars with super powers, especially in third world nations. We long to see every believer in the Body of Christ be activated in the free gifts God offers through His Holy Spirit. We have learned that God desires to impart these free gifts in order that His compassion will work through us and many will be healed and delivered of their sicknesses, diseases, and demonic oppression. This is what Carol and I are committed to do everywhere we go.

Whenever I conduct a gathering of believers, I make sure that I am not the only one praying for people's needs. I pray for those willing believers so that they can lay their hands on people and see them healed. As a result, we have scores of testimonies.

Upper Egypt: Gallbladder Disease

On one of our trips to Egypt, we were invited to Upper Egypt. Before speaking at the church that night, I was in prayer before the Lord, and He gave me a word of knowledge about a woman. I could see how she was dressed and where she would sit in the congregation. During the meeting that night I saw the very woman God had pointed out in my prayer time.

"Madam," speaking through my interpreter and pointing directly to the woman I saw seated in the congregation, "Do you have a gallbladder problem?" I asked. "God wants to heal you." She shook her head "No," explaining that she had no pain in her abdomen.

Well, this is awkward, I thought to myself. Puzzled by her answer I looked around her thinking perhaps I had missed it. Another woman behind her said that she had pain in her abdomen so I asked several around her to pray for her. I prayed a prayer of impartation on the congregation but did not lay hands on her personally.

The next day Carol and I took the long train trip back to Cairo and en route we received a phone call from the pastor on our cell phone.

"Ron, you'll never imagine what happened! Remember the lady you asked if she had a gallbladder problem?" the Pastor asked me.

"Yes," I said, "is she okay?"

"In the middle of the night she developed terrific pain and they rushed her to the hospital," the pastor told me. "It was her gallbladder! She had immediate surgery."

I was stunned! Here God had warned me ahead of time, which I believe was an encouragement to the church. Since we had prayed for each of them to lay hands on sick people, the pastor and his team went to the hospital and did just that.

Finland: Knees Healed

In Finland, God showed me, as I was preparing to minister in a church on Sunday morning, that He was going to heal people. Then He showed me that He would not do it through me; He would heal through a child. When I began the service, I gave out a word of knowledge of those who had pain in their body and several people came forward. All eyes were on me that morning as the congregation fully expected me to lay hands on these individuals and see them healed through the power of the Holy Spirit.

I surprised them by my next announcement: "I would like two children to please come forward." This took a little coaching as Finnish people are not demonstrative and do not like attention drawn to them. Finally, I was able to recruit a young 10-year old girl with blond hair and freckles. She came forward and nervously stood looking at me. Through my interpreter, I assured her that this would be easy and fun and that God was going to heal people because she laid hands on them.

The congregation expectantly leaned forward.

"Now," I instructed the young girl, "lay your hands on that man's knee and repeat after me." She leaned down, placed her hands on the man's knee, and riveted her eyes on me as she readied herself.

"In Jesus' name," I said, and she repeated in Finnish through the translator, "knee be healed!" With this I asked the man to bend his knee and to tell about any change.

What happened next shocked the whole congregation. His face turned beet red as he lifted his hands high in the air. Turning to face the church, he yelled something out in Finnish. The whole place erupted in praise and applause to God.

"What did he say?" I inquired of my interpreter, but I didn't need the translation. The man took off running and then danced around the sanctuary. It was clearly obvious—God had healed his knee through a 10-year old girl!

This proved my point to the members of this church: God wants each person to be filled with His gifts so all may be edified and healed. We really desire the Body of Christ to be equipped long after we leave their nation. That is how to transform a city, a nation.

Texas: Frozen Thumbs Healed

On a trip to Texas, I shared this same directive from the Lord and then invited the congregants to hold out their hands as if they were receiving gifts from God. I prayed a simple prayer of impartation for Him to fill up their hands with His free gifts.

"If someone here needs healing," I called out, "would you stand up where you are? And those around them, just lay your hands on them and command the condition to be healed in Jesus name."

All across the sanctuary people were moving out of their seats, either standing up or positioning themselves to lay hands on the person who needed healing. I joined in praying over the congregation as well. Several people were healed that morning, but one in particular really stood out.

In the meeting was an industrial plumbing engineer

who had been working in construction on the Dallas Cowboys' stadium. In the process of this job, he had contracted Carpal Tunnel Syndrome in both of his hands. As a result, he could not even open a jar or button his own clothes, much less work at his job. Both of his thumbs were literally frozen outside their normal radial range.

As I was greeting people at the end of the service, the assistant pastor came to me and pointed him out. He was standing with his back to the congregation on the platform just praising God, hands raised in the air, and clenching and unclenching his fists over and over again. I went up to speak with him.

"I thought I was always going to be this way," he told me, tears running down his face. "I had completely lost hope of ever regaining normal movement in my thumbs ever again."

At the moment when I was praying a prayer of impartation for the congregation, this man's wife suddenly felt fire in her hands. With this manifestation, she simply laid her hands on her husband; his pain completely disappeared and his thumbs were loosed.

"But look now . . ." We both stood there in awe as he moved his thumbs in circular motions to demonstrate what God had done for him that morning.

Holding up his hands high in the air, he announced, "They are no longer frozen!" Everyone around us erupted in laughter at this God-miracle. The beautiful part of this testimony is that with his thumbs now healed and with full usage of his hands, God had also restored his job. He was elated and so was I.

I called the pastor some time later to check up on the man who was healed. The pastor told me the healing God did on that morning was a hundred percent, allowing the man to fulfill his work responsibilities with no problems whatsoever.

I never cease to marvel at God's amazing love and compassion manifested in such tangible ways. He loves to heal us!

Missouri: Scoliosis Healed

I was with a special gathering of men under the great name "Firecall." We were huddled together praying over one another. A man came to the group and asked for prayer because of pain in his shoulder and hip. I laid one hand on the man's upper back and one hand on his chest as several of us prayed for his healing. After the prayer, my hand on his back slid down to what I felt was a deformity in his spine half way down his back.

"What is that?" I inquired.

"I have scoliosis. I've had it since I was a very small child," he told me. Now I was frantically searching my mind for an appropriate prayer. This was not just a headache or back pain, this was a serious deformity.

While I was asking God what to do, what sort of prayer to pray, out of my own mouth I blurted, "Well, not anymore you don't!" Laying my hands directly on the deformed area of his spine, I prayed and commanded his back to be straightened. It was a bold prayer of faith that came from deep within me without processing or reasoning it out. It was a God-breathed power-prayer as I felt fire in my hands.

Several of the men gathered around me also as we together laid hands on the man and continued to pray. Suddenly, as I was praying for him, I felt a surge of heat in my hands with a distinct shift of the bones where the deformity had been. I literally felt his spine move toward the center!

"Hey! Did you feel your spine move?" I asked him excitedly. Now he was twisting his body around to check it as his whole face brightened in a smile. "Yeah, and my whole body realigned itself!"

"I don't feel that bump any longer," I told him. "Can you feel the change?"

The man was feeling his back with his hand, up and down his spine, and a look of shock came over his face. He bent over, twisting and straightening his newly flexible spine, as everyone erupted in joyous praise to Jesus.

Checking a few weeks later with the pastor, I was excited to hear that this man continued to retain the healing from his lifelong scoliosis condition. More good news is that he now has his own group of men meeting together to grow in God's grace gifts.

Egypt: Back Healing

I was truly expectant for all God had pre-planned for our first trip to Egypt. The first home gathering I addressed was by far the hungriest group of Christians I have yet to meet. They hung onto every word as I spoke, and then wanted to "do" what I had taught. The wife of one of their ministry leaders had severe back pain which required that she be helped in and out of bed. This painful condition had gone on for quite some time. The medical diagnosis and X-rays showed a disc in her lower back was ninety-percent out of place. Her doctor told her it was so critical that she needed emergency surgery.

She held off surgery because she felt God was about to do a miracle in her body. With what I had just shared with this group and after praying a prayer of impartation for God's gifts into their hands, we all caravaned over to her house to lay hands on her, believing in faith.

I was determined to let her family members actually be the ones to lay hands on her to release God's healing.

We spent some time in prayer, and then I sensed the Lord say to my heart, "One of her legs is short."

"Let's check her legs," I suggested to the group, "to see if one leg is shorter than the other." I quickly explained that pain in the back can be the result of uneven legs.

"Why don't you sit in the chair and straighten out your legs so we can see if they are uneven," I suggested. She agreed reluctantly, and sure enough, one was indeed significantly shorter than the other. I was holding up the heels of her legs so all could see.

"Now everyone come and lay hands on her legs," I instructed, "and then command that they grow out and become even." Just as I was speaking those words, her leg popped out. The team saw it and gasped. They were jumping around and backslapping each other. They had never seen this happen before.

Even though our friend saw her leg become even, nothing significant seemed to happen in her back right away. I was a bit disappointed when we left. Her legs were even, but the back pain remained.

We returned to the residence where we were staying for the night and went directly to sleep. About 5:30 in the morning, however, I heard what sounded like a party in the living room. I got up to see what was happening. It was the young woman's husband saying that his wife had literally jumped out of bed that morning without pain for the first time in months! He was so shocked by this that he took her directly to the hospital and made them X-ray her back again.

The doctor was holding up two x-ray films and shaking his head as he asked, "How did you do that?"

"This back is not that back," pointing to the two differing x-rays, "and you no longer need surgery," he announced. "But, how did you do that?" he kept asking.

The family was astonished at the great miracle as they watched God fill up their hands and answer their prayer of faith.

Carol and I see this Jesus culture generation living in a passionate relationship with Him, redefining the Church from powerless to empowered, from limited to infinite. Nothing shall be impossible for those whose lives demonstrate everything is possible if you believe and activate extreme faith.

The King has decreed
good news:

No more veils.
Pre-veil will prevail!

THE GOOD NEWS

We marvel at all that has happened in the Middle East over the past 20 years that we have worked there. So much prayer and travail has been offered up to God's throne on behalf of the peoples of this region. The good news is that the veil is being removed, and the Messiah Jesus is revealing Himself to both Jews and Arabs in supernatural ways through dreams, visions, and miracles. There are websites on the internet and social networks dedicated to sharing publicly the testimonies of these who have encountered Jesus through life-transforming encounters.

Qatar's TV news channel Al-Jazeera, a major news network in the Islamic world, interviewed[72] a noted Imam and Islamic cleric Sheikh Ahmad Al Katani from Libya. His statement

---

[72] Qatar's Al Jazeera TV News interview with Imam Sheikh Ahmad Al Katani, 2003, President of Tripoli's Sharia University.

stunned us. He announced that Africa has been lost to Islam. He went on to tell the interviewer that over 600 Muslims per hour are converting to Christianity from Islam. That is 6,000,000 per year! Think about it: The fastest growing religion in Africa is Jesus of Nazareth, the One crucified and resurrected!

We have met literally scores of people in the Middle East region who have shared their personal testimony with us of how they came to faith in Jesus. In most all of the cases, it was in a sovereign, supernatural vision, a dream, or because God healed their body miraculously. Jesus is appearing to Jews and Muslims in such convincing ways that they are ready to follow Him no matter the personal cost. Many are suffering persecution because of their decisions; some may lose their lives as martyrs.

We have friends who have dedicated their lives to sharing Jesus with Muslims and discipling ex-Muslims committed to following Jesus of Nazareth, the Son of God. There are those who have chosen not to marry even, knowing full well that they could be arrested, tried, and executed for their work of bringing Muslims into the Light of the Gospel. To us, this exemplifies crazy faith.

The good news of the Middle East continues to emerge and excite us. The testimonies of God's goodness poured out to those who are hungry and seeking Him is thrilling. We learned that since the beginning of Egypt's revolution that erupted in 2011, more Muslims have come to faith in Jesus than at any other time. Scores of Muslims are requesting Bibles, going to churches, and boldly inquiring about Jesus from their Christian friends. A shift has taken place in the region. There are churches in Islamic countries now where churches are outlawed! Jesus has appeared to Muslims while on the Islamic pilgrimage camped across from the Ka'aba. This is happening in our time. That should really excite us! There are no closed borders to the Spirit of God revealing Himself to those who are seeking Him. This is true for Jews and Muslims.

We would like to share a testimony from an Islamic country. All the names have been changed to protect these individuals.

Ahmed came to faith through an online website of a former Muslim who also encountered Jesus in a dramatic and personal way. This person contacted us and asked us to meet with Ahmed in his country. The following is a true account of Ron's meeting with Ahmed.

Testimony of a Former Muslim

"What will you change my name to?" came the question from the back seat of the car.

"What?" I responded.

"What will you change my name to when you baptize me?" I was visiting an Islamic nation and joined an underground worker for MBBs (Muslim background believers). We had spent an afternoon with Ahmed.[73] For safety reasons, we met outside of the city where he lived.

Having this one-on-one opportunity to pour into Ahmed was a joy because, as a new believer, he had no theology to unravel. If you said it was Gospel, he believed it. All the great gifts of the abundant life in Jesus he just seemed to swallow whole with great enthusiasm. We simply could not feed him fast enough. We filled him up with Heaven's greatest treasures. It was an afternoon none of us will ever forget.

At the end of our meeting, we left Ahmed at the restaurant where we had met and began our drive back to our home base. Five minutes down the road, Fadi[74] looked at me and said, "Let's go back and baptize him."

---

[73] Not his real name.

[74] Not his real name.

"Can we do that?" I almost shouted with excitement. Being in an Islamic country, I was not sure how one would go about baptizing a former Muslim, now a fiery believer in Jesus.

Fadi flipped open his cell phone and soon I could hear Ahmed almost coming through the phone with excitement. He was thrilled at the opportunity to finally be baptized! The stark contrast is that in the West, we take baptism for granted. But, in an Islamic country, a person who changes their religion from Islam to Christianity through baptism understands that they have crossed the point of no return. The same is true for a Jewish person. For Ahmed, baptism meant full commitment to Jesus and renouncing the religion of his fathers.

We spun the little car around and headed back to pick him up.

"Hey, let's stop and get some juice and crackers to give him his first communion!" I suggested. Fadi agreed with me. This would be the day of full encounter with Jesus.

When we found Ahmed again, he jumped in the back seat, and it was clear he could hardly contain himself with the anticipation. A Muslim baptized into Christianity must change his name!

"I need a Christian name now," Ahmed told us.

At first, I was stunned hearing him ask this, realizing he understood its full implications. I had not even thought of it. I should have, however, after living in the Middle East 20 years. Any life-changing God-encounter event in biblical times was marked and memorialized with a name change: Abram was changed to Abraham, Sarai to Sarah, Jacob to Israel, etc.

I turned to Ahmed in the backseat, intently beholding

him while searching the mind of the God and inquiring of His Spirit who this person was that He had created. When suddenly, I knew it!

"You are Joshua[75]," I declared to him face-to-face, "because you are God's warrior!" I said it with the confidence of a father to a son. It was my blessing over him, and I could see he recognized his God-given identity.

As Fadi negotiated heavy traffic, the little car jostled us as he weaved in and out of lanes. I could see the body posture of Ahmed-now-Joshua change as he settled back in his seat to smell the bouquet of the new name. "Joshua," he played with the sound of his new name.

"Joshua . . . Joshua." A contented smile rested on his face as he leaned against the backseat.

We drove to a safe house deep inside a large city where Fadi often hides MBBs who are in danger from retribution of family members. Fadi's family greeted us warmly at the door with hugs and kisses and welcomed their new brother in the faith.

Upstairs we filled a small bathtub with warm water. Fadi, myself, and Fadi's brother squeezed into the tiny bathroom as Ahmed stepped into the water. He was only able to get on his knees because the tub was so small.

"Joshua," I said, "I baptize you in the name of the Father, and in the name of the Son of God, and in the name of the Holy Spirit." With that I gently put his face down into the water. In that moment, I felt as if we had leaped over centuries where secret baptisms in Jesus' name may have happened in this very region with the early believers under the watchful eyes of the Roman occupation.

Ahmed became Joshua, a confirmed follower of Jesus,

---

[75] Not the real name.

and he rose from the water glowing like Stephen in the book of Acts, "they saw that his face was like the face of an angel."[76] Ahmed went down into the water but came out a new man in Jesus, reborn as Joshua, a warrior on fire.

Before we parted, I prayed that God would fill up his hands with healing, as I had been praying for my other Arabic-speaking Christian friends. Since his baptismal, we have stayed in contact with Joshua thanks to modern technology. In one of our communiqués, Joshua relayed a miraculous story that happened where he works. A client of his had a very bad back. After many medical treatments, he was still not improving. One day, Joshua simply laid hands on their back, commanded it be healed in Jesus' name, and his client was completely healed! They no longer needed medical treatment.

Jesus was confirming to Joshua that His power is working through him, and when he prays for others in His name, He will do it!

Joshua's family knows something spiritually radical has changed in his life, and they are not happy. His family members are ultra-zealous Muslims. Rather than being distressed by family pressures, however, Joshua is strengthening himself in the Lord and writes to us about what Jesus is doing in his heart. This is always the focus of his communications with us, not his sufferings.

Not Loving their Lives unto Death

Joshua knows one day his family may completely reject him because he has been baptized a Christian. One day he wrote us a Scripture that God gave him:

---

[76] Acts 6:15.

When my mother and father forsake me, then the
LORD *will take care of me.* (Psalm 27:10)

Many MBBs have had to go into hiding, spend time in jail, flee their country, and some have lost their lives paying the price to follow Jesus as Lord. When they do experience such sufferings, they find that Jesus embraces them with a supernatural grace. We have not had to pay such a price as believers in other nations do. We have met those who are courageously committed to Jesus and sharing His Word no matter the cost of persecution, jail, or the threat of death by execution for their faith. They are living this Scripture:

And they did not love their lives in the face of death.
(Revelation 12:11b, HCSB)

These are ones who have truly counted the cost and found that Jesus alone is worthy of everything we have to give, including our own lives. The threat of death is not a deterrent to fulfilling the will of God. It's all for love.

And yet, believers like Joshua continue to find ways to demonstrate Jesus in everyday life. Our former Muslim friend lives in a vibrant relationship with Jesus, and the Lord continues to strengthen his faith in Him. The Holy Spirit gives him astounding prophetic dreams as well. Just as our former-Muslim-now-Christian friend Joshua came to faith in a supernatural encounter with Jesus, so too is the Holy Spirit continuing to work through him in supernatural signs, wonders, and miracles. It becomes a natural part of living and walking in a deep friendship with the Father. This is, in fact, the normal Christian life.

The intimacy we share with Jesus—heavenly presence—is so powerful when taken out to the marketplace to radiate among the people. God's heart is always to reach people with His love, and He will cause the power of our intimate union to effect the atmosphere and everyone around us.

"Our Blood Passionately Longs for You!"

On a trip to an Islamic country, I was invited to go with a friend to a Christian hospital where they treat Nubian people who are ill. Carol and I have a particular passion for the Nubian people as they were one of the last tribal peoples to be converted to Islam. They have suffered terribly under the oppressive regimes in the Middle East, and you can see this pain and grief on their faces. As we have gone into this Islamic country, we have prayed that God would return the Nubians to their Christian heritage and restore all that was lost to them. When we were with them, we sensed the deep mourning of their souls and heard Jesus say, "I miss them . . . and they miss Me. Get them back for Me."

We passed a room in the hospital, and I told my young Christian friend George[77] that I felt we should go speak to the patient I could see from the hallway. "I felt that too!" he said. The Holy Spirit confirmed His leading.

We went into the room to find this Nubian Muslim man and his daughter. We requested permission to pray for him as we could see he was very ill; the daughter gratefully agreed. We found out he recently had surgery for prostate cancer. When we finished praying in the name of Jesus, his face was beaming and he was all smiles.

George then began to explain the Gospel to the daughter in Arabic. She interrupted him saying, "You Christians are our cousins . . . and we miss you!" As

---

[77] Not his real name.

George translated for me, he paused to explain the words she had used.

"In Arabic she used words that translate 'we miss you,'" George said. The Nubian desert tribal people, we learned, highly treasure beautiful words and are masterful wordcrafters. They communicate poetically.

"But what she really said," George went on to explain, "was, 'our blood passionately longs for you!'"

Her response was so beautiful, I was simply overcome. This was confirmation to how God had been leading Carol and I to pray for the Nubian tribes.

I said, "Oh George! Let's just pray with them right now to receive Jesus, return them back into the Kingdom...to restore their full inheritance!" I could hardly contain my excitement.

Right there, in that hospital room, my friend George and I led them to Jesus. After the prayer, the daughter said to me, "Peace just descended overwhelming me."

That was proof of His presence! God had given us the first fruits of the very people He put on our hearts a year previous.

The Unveiling

The veil is indeed coming off of the eyes of the Jewish and Muslim people. How will it come off? By the revelation of Jesus and testimony of those who release His love and presence.

For 42 years, Ron and I have lived and worked amongst the Jewish people. I (Carol) count it a great privilege to have been in a ministry to the Jews for so many years. My grandmother's family immigrated to America from Damascus, Syria. And yet, God gave me an unexplainable love for the Jewish people since I was a teenager. I adopted them as my own. Only two years ago the Lord said, "Now, learn Arabic, and go to your people."

My Mother's side is Syrian and my father's family is German heritage. I find it interesting that God chose me from these two people groups to love on the Jewish people for the last 4 decades. I have identified with them in such a deep way, that even my Israeli friends commented, "Carol, you are more Israeli than we are!" I took it as confirmation that my mission of reconciliation as an ambassador of Christ was successful.

I have observed that those who renounce anti-Semitism and choose to bless the Jewish people and the nation of Israel will experience God's far reaching blessings that extend to the entire family. I have seen the curse reversed—even generationally— because one in the family chose to bless the Jews.

God's love is the opposite spirit of centuries-old, demonically-induced hate and prejudice between Jews and Arabs. As I have lived the testimony of loving both Jews and Arabs with my life, prejudices are exposed, and hearts transformed. As Christians, we love without prejudice, which may even go against our national and religious interests or family heritage, but God will honor us with a curse reversal and bring blessing to our family and to our nation. With Jesus' ministry of reconciliation within our hearts, Christian Arabs and Jewish believers in the Middle East work side-by-side in joint efforts. In addition, some Jewish believers receive a love call by the Spirit to Islamic nations. Likewise, Arabic-speaking Christians feel God's heart toward the Jews and even go to Israel. God is up to something huge! He is releasing peace in the Middle East through us, His Church.

This generation will be unveiled as Jesus' passion for all peoples is revealed.

The Children of Isaac and Jacob—the Jews

The Scripture is clear that God allowed a veil to cover the spiritual eyes of the Jewish people for the sake of the Gentiles.

Why? So that these nations would come to Him. But I believe we are living in the time when God is removing that veil completely. As we said, we are hearing more and more testimonies of Jewish people who are receiving a personal revelation of the Messiah in extraordinary ways. The Body of Messiah in Israel and the diaspora[78] is alive and well.

Keep your eyes on the Jewish people in the coming days. For when the veil comes off, the region will experience a spiritual earthquake of biblical proportions.

What will their acceptance be but life from the dead?
(Romans 11:15)

The Veil of Moses vs. the Torn Veil

Paul, a Jew and zealous keeper of the Law, was completely transformed by his face-to-face, supernatural encounter with Jesus the Messiah on the road to Damascus. The glory of the Father shining through the face of Jesus appeared to him and literally blinded his eyes. That same brilliant glory that Moses experienced on Mount Sinai and the disciples experienced on the Mount of Transfiguration, God used to personally remove the veil from Paul's understanding.

For God who said, "Let light shine out of darkness," has shone in our hearts to give the light of the knowledge of God's glory in the face of Jesus. (2 Corinthians 4:6)

Paul refers to this veil of the Old Covenant as "the fading glory."

---

[78] Jewish people living outside of Israel.

Now if the ministry of death, chiseled in letters on stones, came with glory, so that the Israelites were not able to look directly at Moses' face because of the glory from his face—a fading glory—how will the ministry of the Spirit not be more glorious? (2 Corinthians 3:7, 8)

As the Israelites begged Moses to not let God speak to them at Mount Sinai after hearing His voice, God responded by giving them the Law through Moses. His preference, however, was a face-to-face intimate relationship with His people; but they chose the Law which became a veil over their eyes. With Jesus' last words on the Cross, "It is finished," that veil was torn, the entrance into God's presence and the invitation for a personal relationship with Him through Jesus the Messiah was offered once again.

We are not like Moses, who used to put a veil over his face so that the Israelites could not stare at the end of what was fading away, but their minds were closed. For to this day, at the reading of the old covenant, the same veil remains; it is not lifted, because it is set aside only in Christ.

Even to this day, whenever Moses is read, a veil lies over their hearts, but whenever a person turns to the Lord, the veil is removed. (2 Corinthians 3:13-16)

When the Jewish people refused once again the invitation to remove the veil of Moses through Jesus' redemption, the veil remained over their eyes. Once we have beheld the glory of Jesus, however, there is no need—or desire—for religious rituals from the Old Covenant to veil His presence ever again. There were believers in Messiah during Paul's day who remained blinded by the veil of Moses through the Law. His admonition to his Jewish brothers was to remove the veil once and for all and completely trust in the finished work of the Cross through Jesus.

The veil was torn top to bottom on the day of Jesus' crucifixion because Father longs for the intimacy of a face-to-face relationship. At His personal invitation, let us determine to remain unveiled to see Him with clarity and run into the Holy Place of His presence.

Paul's Spiritual Children

During his life, Paul worked tirelessly throughout Israel, pre-Islamic Arabia, Syria, Turkey and modern day Greece to bring the Good News. This region became the central hub of the early Church and Christianity that spread around the world. Some of the oldest churches in the world are in these nations. Even though much of this region is under Islam today, the Church is alive and well. The Christians there are experiencing a deep work by the Spirit of God, and He is strengthening them for the coming harvest. The veil is even coming off of the Orthodox Church. Though the Church in Islamic nations suffers persecution and experiences fewer religious freedoms such as we enjoy in the West, they are receiving strategies of the Holy Spirit and are zealous to expand the kingdom of God throughout the Arabic-speaking world and beyond.

Watch for spiritual explosions in these nations as God restores their full inheritance to empower His Church.

The Children of the Prophet Mohammed

The Church in the Middle East is being equipped to boldly declare God's Word in greater power and strength as never before. Many Arabic-speaking teams are sent to Islamic nations, some even to Israel, to encourage the churches there and boldly declare the Gospel of Jesus. It is our privilege to partner with the Holy Spirit in this as Father is being revealed and to be witnesses of those who have exchanged the veil for an intimate relationship with Him.

Fatima, and all the Daughters of the Prophet

Fatima az-Zahra was the daughter of Mohammed known as the Prophet. Her descendants are treated as royalty in Islam.

One morning, while Ron was ministering in an Islamic country, God awakened me with this word:

> Sweet Fatima
> Singing soft
> All we beside her
> At eventide.

I puzzled about this poetic word God dropped into my spirit until Ron wrote me the following testimony two days later.

Granddaughters of the Prophet

I was asked to be a part of a gathering in an Islamic nation. The meeting had finished, and five of us piled in the car to go home. Still full of the joy of God's presence from the prayer meeting, we were exchanging encouragements back and forth in the wild ride through the night traffic of this bustling Arabic-speaking city. One of the young women in the back seat said to the other girl, "You know, I am one of the great-great-granddaughters of the Prophet Mohammed."

I whirled around to look at her in shock, "What did you say?"

"I am the 38th generation granddaughter of the Prophet Mohammed," she restated.

With this I began to laugh. I was laughing so hard and for so long, the young women in the backseat began to wonder what I thought was so funny. To me, this was the frosting on the cake. Only seven years previous, I had survived a bus bombing in Jerusalem by a radical Islamist who hated Jews. Five years after that, I forgave the suicide bomber from my heart, and God replaced that hate and resentment with love for the Arab people.

Now here I was, in an Islamic country, riding in the car and hearing how one of the offspring of the Prophet Mohammed had been transformed into a radical, on fire, crazy-in-love-with-Jesus Christian! All I could do was laugh, and declare, "Islam does not stand a chance."

Yes, Jesus gets all the spoils of this war.

Carol and I are making declarations about this generation of Muslim young people now:

The children of the Prophet Mohammed belong to Jesus.

All the daughters of Fatima will be unveiled to clearly see the glory of the Father through Jesus His Son.

The Father will visit you in dreams at night and visions in the day to reveal Jesus of Nazareth, His beloved Son.

God has a Son. God has a Son. God has a Son. His name is Jesus of Nazareth.[79]

The Floodgates are Open

With testimonies like these, we see all the elements of revival already here. As more of the Body of Christ begins to activate the gifts the Holy Spirit has given to us as tools to further His kingdom, a flood of His presence will be released in the very regions of the world where we have been crying out for revival, including those unreached. He has already opened the floodgates. Evidence of the Kingdom of God through His people exercising their authority and overwhelming the powers of darkness are certainly stronger in these regions.

The most important advantage of our day, which did not exist in previous revivals, is that we are connected to the world instantly, in real time. We can immediately know what is going on anywhere in the world with an internet or wireless connection. The rapid advancements in technology allow us more advantages for the Gospel than ever before. When this move of God reaches critical mass, the world will be informed within minutes.

There are many who believe God is building an infrastructure for a sustainable revival and love revolution that will be a lifestyle transformation and not just a short-lived visitation. God is raising up the five-star generals in this army, both men and women, and giving them strategies of the Spirit in preparation for regional and global Son-bursts.

We will continue to hear good news from the Middle East despite tensions erupting in the region reported through the

---

[79] This declaration is the exact opposite of the lie declared by Islam that "God has no son", and their false belief in Jesus of Mary of Mecca.

media almost daily. We always say, wherever it seems the darkest, God will explode His brilliance through the Church. How do we know? Because the Father is demonstrating His heart of compassion to all the nations He passionately loves through His transformed lovers.

Stay tuned for *that* good news report.

As
Kingdom ambassadors,
we have been given
love feast assignments:
to the rich and poor,
the highest and lowest,
the best and worst,
the darkest and dirtiest,
the forgotten and ignored
the sick and dying,
the lonely and tormented,
to hell itself.
Compassion feeds them all.
None excluded.
No one is exempt.

THE NEXT MISSION

Not long before this book was published, I (Carol) got a familiar impression: *Go through everything in your house.* I knew in my spirit what that meant. Through our 40 years as a married couple, I have received this same message several times.

Shortly after receiving this impression, it became clear we were to pack it up and move across an ocean. About a week later, we received a phone call from our landlord informing us that the owner of the house we were renting had passed away and they were coming over for an appraisal. That was another clear sign: *Something is up. Stay ready. Stay alert.*

About twenty years ago, Ron and I had been praying and fasting for a week, as we both felt there was a major change coming in our lives. One day during this focused time as I was deep in prayer, there was a knock at the door. When I opened the large special delivery box, I was shocked to see a 7-piece luggage set sent by a family member. No explanation, nothing. I had not said a word to anyone. This was another confirming sign that God was leading us to our next assignment. Within nine months of receiving that luggage set, Ron and I had sold our home in the USA, and our family was repositioned once again back in the Middle East.

During the writing of this book, my husband and I dismantled our home in the United States and returned to live in the Middle East, our third move to the region, and the fifth time we have moved across an ocean to start over. We are presently living and ministering in Egypt.

For 40 years, we worked among the Jewish people, and for twenty of those years, we lived in the State of Israel where we raised our three children. We learned Hebrew and adapted the Israeli culture and Jewish life-cycle of biblical feasts and festivals as our own. Now here we are in this latter season of our lives, excited that God is giving us yet another culture, language, and people group to adopt. With this new mission, we are receiving greater measures of crazy faith and ecstatic joy to partner with the Holy Spirit for all He desires in the region.

With the move came the inevitable questions, "Why would you go there?" followed by, "It is dangerous! Did you see the news today?" and, "How long will you be there? Will you come back soon?" All of these questions represent the caring hearts of those we love, so we do not minimize their concerns. Yet, the life we chose to live with Jesus over forty years ago has led us to make such radical shifts.

We have determined that the vision that drives us into the extraordinary will be as powerful at the end of our lives as it is right now.

Extraordinary Faith

There is really only one thing that draws the attention and

quick response of God, and it is extraordinary faith. This is faith outside of anything that resembles "balance" and stands above the expected "norm". It is, in fact, supernatural faith, the kind that draws on Heaven's resources to respond to the one exhibiting this other-worldly trust in God exclusively. This faith-posture demonstrates, "God will come through . . . I have no other options."

Super faith will look strange; it will cause bystanders to view the person as "crazy" when they hear extraordinary faith declarations and trust in God exercised for provision, healing, miraculous intervention, and direction. This faith-crazed person will be accused of praying and acting presumptuously. Yet, this is exactly what God is looking for in each one of us. It is the kind of faith in Him that says, "You can do anything, so I trust You for that! I put myself completely and wholly in Your hands. I will go anywhere and do anything, so long as Your name is known in the earth. For this, I look only to You, Lord." By most religious standards, that's just crazy.

Yes, yes, it is. Extraordinary faith. Abraham displayed such faith. In fact, Hebrews chapter eleven lists many heroes of faith who got His full-on attention.

Jesus always pointed out people He encountered who had little faith, no faith, and those who displayed extraordinary faith. The latter are the ones who encountered God supernaturally and wrought great miracles and exploits to the glory of God.

We want that kind of attention from God.

Hell's Final Push

In our day, we will need this kind of crazy faith and extraordinary love to match what we will be facing. It is for sure satan's hordes will be running headlong towards God's people in fierce opposition. We are equipped to match it with the spirit of Heaven, the exact opposite of hell's fury against us. The enemy has no tools against the Spirit's arsenal of power as we release firebrands of love, faith, compassion, joy, peace, etc.

Satan has been preparing a final, wholly-committed generation to go up against us. Its run-up is the "Harry Potter" generation. Our culture has been baptized into witchcraft and the demonic realm so that it has dulled us to its potent, spirit-draining intentions. So much so that we hardly even notice its effects all around us. It will only be increased in the days ahead.

How will the Church more than match the unleashing of Hell which has saved its greatest onslaught for our last generation? Those who walk in deep intimacy with Jesus, and His authority, will release the powerful demonstrations of the Spirit of God. Hell's hordes withdraw in defeat at the power of passion exchanged and released between the Beloved and the lover. This army of Jesus lovers, oozing God's love through uncommon expressions, is the uncontested victor no matter what Hell has prepared against them. They are unstoppable, and no hell hole is too dark to find and release its captives into freedom.

Our friend, Matti Arnold, represents this wholly committed generation of lovers who have chosen to live in the ecstacy of Heaven's love and joy. These are the commissioned ones. He recently sent us an entry from his personal journal that fully expresses his heart and exemplifies this generation captivated by passion for Jesus.

Ecstasy of Love[80]

There is a reality of love, a realm and a dimension that is so, so, so, so powerful that once you walk into it, you don't leave the same. In this reality, everything that would stand in the way of love (hurt, bitterness, shame,

---

[80] Arnold, Matti. Journal entry, unedited. Copyright 2010. Used by permission.

guilt, offense, fear, insecurity, abandonment, confusion and anything else), melts away. It crumbles up, it burns up, it blows away. In this place, the very core of what we are made of catches on fire and we are changed by the intensity of the heat of goodness.

So few people even know of this place, and those who find it stay there as long as they can, until even they cannot handle the intensity of it and crawl out of it on their hands and knees. Some, unfortunately never go back; they place limitations on themselves and listen to illusionary fears that have no authority.

Yet there are others who choose to go back again and again and again, and others who choose to move themselves there, and they will live in this reality for the rest of their blissful and incomprehensible days.

These are the ones who the world does not and cannot understand. They sojourn the globe looking for the darkest, saddest cave of depressed souls they can find. They purposefully climb into the pit of rusty nails with the zombies who live in them just to get a chance to hug them and release the power of love on them. The darker the situation or the individual, the better the target to love because the reality they live in is so powerful, it consumes the dark shadows of the sad people who cry themselves to sleep, like a light bulb consumes darkness effortlessly.

Effortlessly.

Effortlessly these ecstatic's pour themselves out for any and everyone around them with selfless love and compassion, because the effort it takes to love the "dead and the ugly" (as others call them), is not comparable to the voltage of their joy.

It's not enough to reach down to the dead kids who lay on the cold sewage and try to pick them up. They dive into the poop themselves, joyfully pressing their own bodies against the broken glass in the sewer to lift up the dying ones from below.

The by-product or the "exhaust" of their life is joy.

The result of allowing their love to land on the ground is an explosion of joy. Like hydrogen bombs of joy they change the landscape of any place they go. The very atmosphere around them is shifted just when they walk in the room, affecting everyone in their proximity.

They have the fragrance of a different world on them. Those who have never been to the dimension (or realm of love) cannot help but enjoy the sweet smell on them that stirs the senses they never knew they had.

Best of all this sweet and spicy smell that lingers in the room long after the ecstatic leaves, becomes the very appetizer that leads the lonely ones into the same encounter of love that in turn changes them.

And the cycle of crazy love begins again—this time even more powerful than ever before . . . until the kid who used to cry himself to sleep every night, in the agony of his pain, begins to cry himself to sleep with tears of joy.

Heaven's Final Word

Jesus announced His own mandate from Heaven as He began His ministry:

> *The Spirit of the Lord GOD is upon Me, because the LORD has anointed Me to bring good news to the poor. He has sent Me to heal the brokenhearted, to proclaim liberty to the captives and freedom to the prisoners;*

*to proclaim the year of the LORD'S favor, and the day
of our God's vengeance; to comfort all who mourn,
to provide for those who mourn in Zion; to give
them a crown of beauty instead of ashes, festive oil
instead of mourning, and splendid clothes instead
of despair.* (Isaiah 61:1-3, HCSB)

Jesus' mandate of proclaiming Jubilee is also our mandate; it was never withdrawn. His anointing on us releases the full freedoms of Jubilee already proclaimed and guaranteed by His blood. From here on, life is declared and released where death once reigned. This is the Gospel, and it is Heaven's final word.

Healed of Cancer

A friend in our northern California neighborhood received the distressing diagnosis from his doctor of throat cancer. All of us rallied around him as we began to contend for his healing. We took up our position before the Lord in prayer and adoration. Our friend had opted for radiation and not the severe surgical treatment. Many people were also praying for his healing. One day, Carol and I went to his home and asked if we could have a time to pray with him. For about 30 minutes, Carol worshiped and sang over our friend. At one point as she sang, he laid his head against me and wept like a child and I comforted him as a father. I felt God the Father touching him in a profound way.

Over the coming weeks, he received the amazing news we had all prayed for: his cancer was completely gone! We had a joyous, celebratory birthday party for him.

We love to see God release full liberties into a person who is suffering so terribly in his body, soul, or spirit. When Jesus spoke His final words, "It is finished," from the cross, He really meant it. The blood of Jesus cleansed us and provided all we need to be forgiven, healed, delivered, set free, and overflowing with God's favor, peace, prosperity, and joy.

Getting God's Full Attention

Crazy faith is what attracts God to you. I (Ron) have perceived in my spirit the rushing of God. I have felt the wind of His presence like a hurricane of fire as never before in my 43 years of relationship with Him and full time vocational ministry. I see God responding to the reception of His outpouring in recent years by literally tens of thousands of people, both young and old. Acts of faith at levels heretofore unseen are the fruit of that response.

Jesus wondered aloud if He would find faith on the earth at His return. The parable in Luke 18 is about a judge who was neither just, religious, nor compassionate. Jesus' parable is not suggesting that God is like this judge. Rather, it is drawing a contrast, wherein He uses the word "swiftly" to describe His Father's dispensation of justice: a rushing swiftness on the part of the Father to embrace His children.

Jesus ends the parable with a question.

> *Nevertheless, when the Son of Man comes, will He find faith on the earth?* (Luke 18:8)

I am answering this question with a resounding declaration, "Yes! Jesus, You will find faith here upon the earth."

Faith is an unearthly commodity. Faith has a little characteristic that spawns more faith. For instance, when a testimony of faith is relayed to others, faith enters the hearer, and like a virus, invades its host with the goodness of God allowing him or her to see Heaven more clearly and act upon what they see. That is the very reason for chapter eleven of the book of Hebrews. The testimonies of the faith of the patriarchs listed there is to elevate us to a level where we could not see any other way. Retelling the testimonies of God's goodness today boosts our courage with a determination to live each moment full of faith so as to attract God's full on attention. Let's do that.

All for Love

What Jesus is doing in the earth right now is being relayed all over the globe. Cyberspace is alive with the testimony of Jesus. Prophecy is to cause Earth to see Heaven as it really is and relay what is happening there. Thus, the Revelation given to John on Patmos . . . see Heaven, see what God is doing, and be transformed.

> *The testimony of Jesus is the spirit of prophecy.*
> (Revelation 19:10)

The revelation given to John is not about what the enemy is doing; it is about what God is doing to the enemy. There is no war—no true contest—between God and satan; God is sovereign. He has always been in control and will always be in control. With that in mind, we can live with the atmosphere of Heaven on us and operate at a level of extreme faith.

It is a big risk to function above a level of expected normalcy, but our hearts are carried away with passion for Him and we long to see His name glorified in all the earth. We take our cues from those who have gone before us and the fiery trail they left in their wake. Their love for Jesus took them into dangerous places where their very lives were threatened and it seemed like the whole city was against them.

The book of Acts is a good example: one scene after another of upheaval, towns being turned upside down, demons evacuating their hosts in a fury, mobs ready to stone the disciples, and people being healed everywhere by such incredible power demonstrations as Peter's shadow and Paul's apron. Philip vanishes from the pool of water in which he had just baptized the Ethiopian eunuch. Shipwrecks and snake bites abound with the apostles taking it all in stride. *What did their families think?*

Paul left a stunning career as an educated rabbi of the highest rank to spend years in the desert at the behest of an apparition which appeared to him on the road to Damascus. Roman-born and quite set for a successful life of the Jewish religious elite, he gave it all to see the Master and be changed. Paul did not look back.

I'm sure his family back home was saying, *Saul, we sent you to the best colleges . . . why are you wasting your life?* But, there was no comparison, no cost, and no loss when measured against all he received for what he gave. Paul's passion for Jesus compelled him.

In every congregation there are concentric circles of faith. There are those who are merely there for fire insurance, dignified and respectable. Then there are those who know they are in a spiritual battle; they are the fighting troops. There are generals who equip those troops. They are not always in leadership, nor should they be; it is the job of the troops to equip one another. Then there are 5-star generals who supply the generals who are training the troops. The 5-stars have their heads in the third Heaven and keep them there. They drink from the full river of God and impart it to the troops on Earth to encourage, refresh, and empower.

Such is the extraordinary faith that attracts Jesus. He comes like a mighty, rushing wind with overpowering presence to embrace the reward of His suffering—you!

Yes, you are the reward of the God of Heaven who seeks to be astounded by your crazy faith. He planned it from before the foundation of the earth.

Astound Him!

About the Authors

Ron and Carol Cantrell have served over forty years in ministry, with more than twenty of those years in the Middle East. Through Immanuel Associated Ministries, Inc., they are partnering with churches and ministry leaders internationally who are passionate for God's presence to be powerfully released for spiritual breakthroughs, transformation, and global revival.

As artists, both Ron and Carol communicate their passion for Jesus through creative expressions of music, art, writing, dance, and drama, creating an environment for His manifested presence.

Ron and Carol are ordained ministers through their home church, The Mission Church, in Vacaville, California. They have three children and six grandchildren.

Presently based in Egypt, they seek to encourage, equip, and train believers as well as partner with God's purposes for the region.

More Resources from Ron Cantrell

Other Books authored by Ron Cantrell and available on Amazon.com :

- *The Feasts of the Lord*
- *The Final Kingdom*

Artwork by Ron Cantrell

Prints of artwork are available for sale
at: FineArtAmerica.com
Search for "Ron Cantrell"

More Resources from Carol Cantrell

Music CDs by Carol Cantrell available on iTunes

- Songs of Zion
- Shalom Shalom Jerusalem

Artwork by Carol Cantrell

Prints of paintings are available for sale
at: FineArtAmerica.com
Search for "Carol Cantrell"